The Fifth-Century A.D. Treasure from Pietroasa, Romania, in the light of recent research

Radu Harhoiu

translated from the Romanian by
Nubar Hampartumian

BAR Supplementary Series 24
1977

British Archaeological Reports

122, Banbury Road, Oxford OX2 7BP, England

GENERAL EDITORS

A. C. C. Brodribb, M.A.
Mrs. Y. M. Hands

A. R. Hands, B.Sc., M.A., D.Phil.
D. R. Walker, M.A.

B.A.R. Supplementary Series, 24, 1977: "The Fifth-Century A.D. Treasure from Pietroasa, Romania, in the light of recent research"

© Radu Harhoiu, 1977

The author's moral rights under the 1988 UK Copyright, Designs and Patents Act are hereby expressly asserted.

All rights reserved. No part of this work may be copied, reproduced, stored, sold, distributed, scanned, saved in any form of digital format or transmitted in any form digitally, without the written permission of the Publisher.

ISBN 9780904531725 paperback

ISBN 9781407340852 e-book

DOI https://doi.org/10.30861/9780904531725

A catalogue record for this book is available from the British Library

This book is available at www.barpublishing.com

CONTENTS

	Page
Foreword	1
CHAPTER 1	
The Chronology and Ethnic Attribution of the Treasure	3
CHAPTER 2	
The Component pieces of the Pietroasa Treasure	7
CHAPTER 3	
The Polychrome Style	19
CHAPTER 4	
Links with other cultural groups	23
CHAPTER 5	
The Historical background	29
Conclusion	36
Notes	37
Appendix	52
Abbreviations	56
Figures and Plates	59

In memory of Professor Ion Nestor

FOREWORD

The present work represents a revised version of my study "Tezaurul de la Pietroasa în lumina noilor cercetari" published in Alexandru Odobescu, Opere vol. IV. Tezaurul de la Pietroasa, Editura Academiei, Bucharest, 1976, pp. 1011-1054, which is the first of three volumes (IV, V, VI) of a critical edition of Odobescu's work, devoted to his historical studies. The full version of Odobescu's works, dealing with the Pietroasa treasure, has been reprinted in this volume, namely his papers:

Studie asupra tezaurului de la Pietroasa, a series of studies, interrupted after four years, in Columna lui Traian (1876-77).

Le trésor de Pétrossa. Notice descriptive et historique, unfinished edition, Paris 1885.

Le trésor de Pétrossa. Historique-Description. Étude sur l'orfévrerie antique, Paris, 1889-1900.

A series of documents reflecting the efforts of Odobescu to obtain the means with which to publish the monographs devoted to the Pietroasa treasure have also been published, partly in Odobescu's lifetime (Pia Desideria, and the correspondence from 1887 with the minister D. A. Sturza), and the rest (the correspondence from 1884 with the minister Titu Maiorescu and an undated petition) are printed for the first time now. The rest of Odobescu's studies belonging to the shorter version, will be published in the next volume of the critical edition devoted to his works (Opere Vol. V).

Taking into account the value of the unfinished edition, and of the definitive edition in French, both monuments of typographical art, they have been photographically reproduced, so as to be, compared with the previous edition, faithful to the original. The volume is accompanied by an introductory study: Odobescu si tezaurul de la Pietroasa (pp. 5-40), and commentary and critical notes referring to the text of Odobescu (pp. 949-1012) made by Mircea Babeş, the editor of the volume. In addition to my study the work comprises also Castrul de la Pietroasa (pp. 1055-1072) by Gheorghe Diaconu which is devoted to the presentation of the main results of the archaeological research carried out in the fortification of Pietroasa (fourth century A.D.) in recent years.

At present the treasure is exhibited in the History Museum of the Socialist Republic of Romania, and has the following inventory numbers: the plate inv. 11426; oenochoe-jug, inv. 11430; patera inv. 11427; eight-sided cup inv. 11428; twelve-sided cup inv. 11429; plain collar inv. 11436; collar with hinge 11437; collar with hinge inv. 11435; small fibula inv. 11434; medium fibulae inv. 11432 and 11433; large fibula inv. 11431.

Radu Harhoiu

CHAPTER 1

THE CHRONOLOGY AND ETHNIC ATTRIBUTION OF THE TREASURE

On the basis of a detailed investigation carried out during the period when archaeology was still lacking a methodology,[1] Odobescu reached the following conclusions with regard to the treasure of Pietroasa (at present Pietroasele).[2]

1. The pieces of treasure belonged to a pagan Germanic people, very likely to the Goths who inhabited Dacia in the 3rd-5th centuries A.D.

2. Not all the pieces date from the same period, but they do show an 'indigenous' art of the Goths from Dacia.

3. The whole hoard belonged to some pagan temple, since it consisted exclusively of sacred vases and sacerdotal ornaments.

According to Odobescu the hoard must have belonged to Athanaric and was buried before the departure of the Visigothic king to Constantinople where he died in 381. In consequence of this the treasure was buried before 381 and the component pieces date from the 4th century A.D.

Many researchers of the following period agreed with these conclusions and the monograph of Odobescu is still a work of reference for the specialist in the period of the migrations.

The Pietroasa treasure has long attracted the attention of specialists, archaeologists, linguists and art historians, both before and immediately after the publication of Odobescu's work; according to their view-point and conception of the cultural and historical traits of the Late Roman Empire, these scholars put forward different theses with regard to the chronological, ethnic and cultural problems aroused by the Pietroasa hoard.

A large number of researchers at this time followed the same line as Odobescu. C. Diculescu,[3] considered in a general history of the Vandals and Goths in Hungary and Romania that the treasure was buried by Athanaric before his departure to Constantinople and supported his opinion only with historical arguments connected with the last years of the presence of Athanaric to the North of the Danube. The majority of the scholars who supported or support the Athanaric hypothesis have taken into account only the historical information of the written records and do not pay attention to the archaeology which can produce conclusive evidence with regard to the chronology, and cultural and ethnic attribution of an archaeological monument; the interpretation of the archaeological sources must be based only on archaeological arguments.[4]

M. C. Soutzo[5] in a small article referring especially to the patera and published in 1932, has a similar opinion as regards the chronology and ethnic attribution of the whole treasure but contrary to the opinion of Odobescu that the figures on the patera represented German gods, Soutzo considered that "the circular assembly of gods round the base of the statuette (Cybele) probably comprise the main native deities of the barbarians who inhabited Dacia before the arrival of the Romans and who then settled into the Olympus of the period". These are confused ideas without any evidence for them.

Gogo Müller Kuales, in an extensive archaeological synthesis of the German tribes, considered the Pietroasa hoard ("The Athanaric treasure" as he calls it) as being the treasure of the whole Gothic people which was buried after the defeat of Athanaric.[6]

J. Werner, in 1956,[7] also assigned the treasure to the 4th century A.D., before the Hunnic invasion; but his opinion also is not based on an archaeological study of the component pieces.

The Athanaric hypothesis, which attributed the treasure to the Visigoths of the 4th century, has been supported by several Romanian specialists since the Second World War. Ecaterina Dunăreanu-Vulpe in 1956 and later in 1967[8] also assigned the treasure to the 4th century A.D. and identified it with the wealth of some king (Athanaric) or of a high priest. In spite of the fact that the author dealt with previously published works which could also lead to other conclusions, especially concerning the chronology, she continued to maintain this thesis. Ion Nestor, in 1960[10] and Răzvan Theodorescu, in 1967,[11] also assigned the treasure to the period of Athanaric.

The burial of hoards consisting of gold ingots (Crasna, Feldioara)[12] or of silver ornaments (Valea Strîmbă) dating from about 380 is one of the arguments produced in support of the thesis that the treasure of Pietroasa was hidden in the time of Athanaric.[14] The hoard of ornaments from Valea Strîmbă consists of pieces of silver which have no stylistic link with the Pietroasa treasure and for this reason, in my opinion, it is not possible to explain the burial of both hoards as a consequence of the same event, namely the Hunnic invasion. N. Fettich showed 40 years ago that the hoards of ingots from Crasna and Feldioara represented the first form of the accumulation of gold by the German tribes living to the North of the Danube, as a result of the situation arising in the Balkan Peninsula after the battle of Adrianople;[15] the fact that this gold was not used for making ornaments could argue in favour of the burial of these hoards in consequence of the Hunnic invasion, although the hypothesis of a later burial has been put forward.[16] In any case we do not believe that the date of the burial of these hoards of ingots, which are up to now unique finds in the Carpatho-Danubian area, can be connected with the date of the burial of the Pietroasa treasure, which from the artistic and stylistic point of view reflects a completely different period.

On the other hand, the relative scarcity of gold coins from the end of the 4th century and the first half of the 5th century[17] could suggest that the gold (coins, ingots or other precious objects) arriving from the Empire was used for the manufacture of splendid ornaments in the 5th century A.D.

W. F. Volbach in a beautifully illustrated but very general work on the art of the period of migrations published in 1967 dates the treasure to the second half of the 4th century, and suggests that the hoard belongs to the first phase of the Pontic art of inlay which ends its development in about 450.[18] The lack of any kind of argument for the dating of the treasure to the second half of the 4th century A.D. prevents us from criticising it.

The work of Birgitt Arrhenius published in 1971[19] produces more conclusive arguments for the dating of the treasure to the 4th century A.D. On the basis of gems and ornaments decorated with garnets found in Northern Europe, the Swedish scholar presents a detailed study of the different technical methods used for the manufacture of ornaments in the 5th-7th centuries A.D. This work is perhaps the most extensive analysis of the techniques of the polychrome style.

According to Arrhenius the absence of garnets cut in the shape of steps (stuffengeschnittene Granate) and of the crystalline mass used as a backing for the stones both, in her opinion, typical of the period of Attila, are the principal arguments against the dating of the treasure to the 5th century. As we will attempt to show later, garnets cut in the shape of steps are not typical only of the first half of the 5th century and the composition of the backing of the pieces from the Pietroasa treasure is the same as that of several objects of the 5th century.

Recently R. Theodorescu in a general work on the art of the Northern-Danubian territory in the first millennium considers the treasure of Pietroasa as "a monument of barbarian art from the end of the 4th century and the beginning of the 5th century" and attributes it to the Goths. The author believes (this idea seems to me inexplicable) that the treasure was buried in about the last decades before 400,[21] and that it means in fact that the concealment of the hoard is connected with Athanaric.

Rostovtzeff differed somewhat from the partisans of the Athanaric hypothesis. Although Rostovtzeff eventually admitted the attribution of the hoard to Athanaric, he considered that the Goths took the whole treasure from a Sarmatian or Thracian prince and then placed the runic inscription on the collar.[22]

This unique opinion, explained by the fact that Rostovtzeff was much preoccupied with Scytho-Sarmatian art, was not adopted by other scholars.

The first opinion dating the treasure to the period after the departure of Athanaric to Constantinople was published at about the time of the first World War.[23]

N. Beleaev, in a study based especially on the literary sources concerning the different types of fibulae in use at the court of the Late Roman and Byzantine Empire, dates the small brooch from Pietroasa to the 5th century and admits the possibility of its circulation also in the next century.[24] The dating of the small brooch to after the first half of the 5th century is implausible, but the conclusion of Beleaev that the brooches with pendants and of similar design to those from Pietroasa do not appear before Valens and are common in Theodosian times is supported, as we will show later, by clear evidence.

On the basis of typological analysis of the brooches from the Pietroasa treasure and of those from the great hoard discovered at Simleul Silvaniei, both A. Alföldi[25] and N. Fettich[26] were inclined to date the Pietroasa hoard to the end of the 4th century and the beginning of the next century.

C. Daicoviciu was the first Romanian archaeologist who dated the Pietroasa treasure to the 5th century and attributed it to the Ostrogoths. Unfortunately, he did not produce documentary evidence in support of his theories.

The research carried out after World War II has produced new arguments for the hypothesis that the Pietroasa treasure dates from a later period. In addition to the rich archaeological material brought to light in this time new methods of investigation will lead to new interpretations concerning several problems of the period of the migrations. Thus, H. Arbman attempted to explain the cultural and historical significance of the swords found in the grave of Childeric.[28] The analogies drawn by H. Arbman[29] between the hilt of the sword from Altlussheim and the collar with hinge from Pietroasa will provide a convincing argument for the later dating, but the author does not put forward hypotheses concerning the chronology and the ethnic attribution of the Pietroasa hoard.

K. Böhner,[30] dealing with the typology of the princely swords from the 5th-7th centuries, firmly dates the Pietroasa treasure to the 5th century on the basis of analysis of the polychrome style of its component pieces.

W. Holmquist, in his work on Germanic art in the first millennium A.D., endorses this dating, on the basis of the same arguments as those of W. Böhner. Neither of these scholars discusses the ethnic attribution of the treasure since they were not dealing with that problem.

K. Horedt,[31] in a brief article published in 1969,[32] (probably written in consequence of the discovery and study of the princely hoard from Someșeni and of the princely tomb II from Apahida,[33] resumes the discussion of the date of the Pietroasa treasure in the 5th century.[34] According to K. Horedt, the cloisonné technique in which the collar with hinge, the multiangular cups, the small brooch and the neck of the large brooch are worked, the presence of the gold collar with hook, in addition to the practice of hoarding vessels of precious metal, are arguments for dating the Pietroasa treasure to the 5th century. On the basis of this dating, Horedt considers that the treasure belonged to the Ostrogoths and its burial must be connected with the events which took place about 450 and which finally led to the fall of the Hunnic Empire.[35]

CHAPTER 2

THE COMPONENT PIECES OF THE PIETROASA TREASURE

The Pietroasa treasure, like the majority of groups of antiquities of this kind, was subject to the law of accumulation, as Odobescu pointed out long ago. In consequence of this accumulation the treasure contains pieces from different periods and which reflect varied cultural traits. For the chronology, the recent pieces are the most conclusive. We can only speculate as to the circumstances of accumulation, of which we often have insufficient literary evidence. The analysis of the pieces of the treasure will attempt, even if partially, to answer some of these questions.

From the point of view of the technique of working, we can distinguish two categories among the pieces intended for a ceremonial purpose (the so-called "sacred vessels" of Odobescu), namely pieces worked only in gold and pieces decorated in a polychrome style.

The most simple and unskilfully made piece in the treasure is illustrated in Plate 1. The whole piece and its decoration is worked in the <u>au repoussé</u> technique by hammering and lightly chasing.

The plate (weight 7.130 kg, diameter 0.56 m) is made of a slightly dished sheet and has a broad (approximately 5 cm) everted rim and a foot-ring. The rim is decorated with simple geometrical patterns in relief, with zig-zag lines bordered by two rows of semi-spherical dots. The angles of these lines are vertically hatched. A fine ribbing with the ends winding in spirals defines the groups of hatching. The decoration in relief on the centre of the plate consists of a rosette with elongated petals enclosed by a band consisting of wavy lines. Some remote parallels can be drawn with the gold plaque found in the tumulus at Certomlîk or with some Roman sarcophagi of the Late Roman period (the 3rd-6th centuries).[37] The decoration does not help us to date the piece more exactly. Rosette is an ordinary decorative pattern in ancient metal-working, and the winding band or the wavy lines are encountered from the Bronze Age to the 9th century A.D., (e.g. the Sînnicolaul Mare treasure); but the small floral details which occur together with the zig-zag lines could be considered as a chronological indication for the period of migration.[38]

The inferior quality of execution can be an argument in favour of the hypothesis that the plate was a local creation, although it has been interpreted as a product of the North-Pontic workshops which used decorative patterns typical of the migratory populations.[39]

The existence of a local craft of metalworking in North-Eastern Muntenia is supported by the discovery of a mould for casting ornaments at Aldeni (district of Buzău), not far from Pietroasa; for analogies can be drawn between this mould and the gold appliqué from the Pîrscov treasure,[40] dating from the first half of the 5th century.[41]

The present form of the jug (oenochoe) (Pl. II) is the result of two restorations. The height is 36 cm, and the form ovoid. The body and the squat foot-ring are linked by a flattened sphere, and the funnel shaped mouth has a horizontally everted rim. Hemispherical pellets are soldered on the lip of the jug. A horizontal plate with opus interrasile decoration representing volutes and stylized bird-heads is held on the lip by rivets. The handle consists of a vertical plain bar, which is rectangular in section. Its thin lower part ends in a spiral and is attached to the vessel by a rivet. A small plate cut in the shape of an acanthus-leaf is held between this spiral and the side of the vessel. The upper part of the handle has a sharp angle and joins the pierced plate and ends in the shape of a bird. The decoration is arranged in zones. The middle zone is decorated with parallel and wavy flutings (strigiles). The other zones are engraved. The basic decorative pattern is represented by stylized acanthus-leaves, and triangles appear on some of the empty spaces between the acanthus-leaves. Rows of small triangles border the zones of the upper part and a band consisting of imbrications their base. Similar imbrications are also engraved on the pierced plate on the mouth of the vessel. The border of the foot-ring is decorated with soldered granules.

A very close analogy can be drawn between this type of vase and the silver jug from the treasure found at Kerch (Hospital Street) on 24 June 1904. That deposit is dated by a dish decorated with the bust of the emperor Constantius II (337-361). The inscription engraved on the dish D[omini] N[ostri] Constanti Augusti votis XX, indicates the vicennalia of Constantius II in 343.[42]

For a more precise dating we must also take into account the other graves discovered on Hospital Street in Kerch. We refer to the catacomb graves No. 145 dated by a coin of Valentinian II (375-392), No. 154 dated by a coin of Valentinian I (364-375), and the grave, not belonging with the others, found on 24 June 1904 and dated by coins of Constantius Gallus (351-354), and Valentinian I and II (364-392).[43] In the light of these finds dating from the end of the 4th century we suggest that the pottery deposit discovered at Kerch can also be dated to the second half of the 4th century.

Other arguments based on the analysis of the decoration of the jug from Pietroasa lead to the same conclusion. We refer especially to the engraved decoration consisting of lines and incised dots arranged in the shape of stylized acanthus-leaves with triangles between them. Since the technique is somewhat alien to the Late Roman workshops, some researchers have considered workshops of the barbaricum as a possible origin of these pieces.[44]

We think rather of the North-Pontic workshops which worked for the "barbarian" population, considering the analogy of the jug from Kerch. The analogies between the decoration on the neck of the jug from Pietroasa and the decoration of the pendants from Coşovenii de Jos (Fig. 1:2,6) which show the same stylized acanthus flower executed in the same technique,[45] indicates a fairly precise date, namely 400.[46] The main decoration of the jug is represented by the strigils, worked in the au repoussé technique, which are arranged on the whole belly of the vessel. This decorative pattern occurs also in Scythian art,[47] then in Roman art and continues to appear in the 6th century as is attested by the discovery of a silver vessel decorated in the same technique at Novobaiazid (Armenia) and which, according to the mark on the base of the vessel, is dated to the time of Justinian I (527-565).[49]

In conclusion we can assert with sufficient certainty that both the analogy with the vessel from the deposit discovered at Kerch, which, according to the coin-finds in the other archaeological complexes situated in its immediate vicinity, must be dated to a late period, and the decoration engraved on the neck of the vessel, can be considered as sufficient arguments in favour of the hypothesis that the vessel from Pietroasa dates from the end of the 4th century, more precisely from about 400.

The presence of pottery vessels within the Sîntana de Mureş-Cerneahov culture which would be copies in clay of the jug from Pietroasa is an argument for an earlier dating, in the course of the 4th century A.D.[50] We refer particularly to the jug discovered as an isolated find at Racoviţa (district of Buzău) in 1943-1945,[51] or to the fragmentary jug belonging to cremation grave no. 18 found at Tîrgsor, district of Prahova.[52] There are no details concerning the context in which the jug was found at Racoviţa, but as regards the jug from Tîrgsor, we know that a pit dated by a bronze fibula with incurved foot to the 4th century A.D.[53] (probably about 350) cut through grave no. 18, and for this reason the jug can be dated to the first half of the 4th century. However, these analogies are not convincing for the dating of our piece. In addition to the fact that the analogy with the jug from Pietroasa is not perfect, the prototypes of metal and even of glass were also imitated at the beginning of the 5th century, as is attested (besides other evidence) by the flagon-jug found in the princely tomb from Regöly; this piece, modelled in grey fabric with black colour coat and with the upper part of the body in facets, like all the pottery jugs under discussion, has the neck ending in a stylized eagle head.[54] The same pattern is encountered on the pierced plate which encloses the lip of the vessel from Pietroasa.

We will deal with the problem of the adoption of the animal pattern in the Carpatho-Danubian area when we consider the clothing accessories which are represented by the fibulae in the shape of eagle-heads.

The _Patera_ (Pl. III-VI) is the sole piece which is hardly damaged. Its height is 7.5 cm and diameter 25.7 cm and it is of concave form and with a small ring-foot. A statuette, which overtops by 3.7 cm the height of the dish, rises in the centre of the patera. The sides of the dish consist of two sheets joined with solder on the border; the outside sheet is flat, while the inside one is richly decorated in relief.

The central figure, modelled in _ronde-bosse,_ represents a seated woman (Pl. IV). The round and backless throne is bordered on the upper and lower sides by a twisted band and is decorated with a vine stalk with leaves and grapes. A narrow frieze around the statuette decorates the bottom of the dish. The central statuette and the figures of this frieze have been separately worked and applied by soldering onto the dish. The rest of the decoration is worked in the _au repoussé_ technique.

A broad zone, enclosed by two twisted cordons, is decorated with a row of human figures in different attitudes (Pl. V-VI). A continuous and circular narrow frieze decorated with stalks of vine with leaves and grapes, some of them hanging over the twisted cordon, and others under this cordon, in the zone decorated with figures, runs between the upper twisted cordon and the rim of the dish, defined by two cordons, one plain, and the other consisting of dots. Three seated figures, arranged with a fairly equal distance between them, separate the other standing figures into three groups.

According to some opinions the patera must be associated with the late Sarmatians from Southern Russia. In conformity with this thesis the central seated figure has a close connection with the Great Goddess venerated by the Scythians and several analogies can be drawn with the Sarmatian phalerae from that area.[55] According to N. Fettich the patera from Pietroasa, together with the cauldron from Gundestrup or with the dish-bowl from Simleul Silvaniei, would belong to the same cultural circle which could be connected with the bowls of Omphalos type from the 5th-6th centuries.[56] The opinion of Soutzo,[57] that the patera represents a Daco-Roman pantheon, remains an isolated and unique hypothesis.

Many scholars following the thesis put forward by Odobescu consider that the figures on the patera represent "most probably a syncretism between deities proper to the German populations, and those of the classical Graeco-Roman world".[58]

Ch. de Linas put forward a hypothesis which differed from this, what was to become the traditional opinion, but he was refuted by Odobescu. According to de Linas the figured scene represents a fancy-dress procession of an Isiac <u>thiasos</u> round the Mother-Goddess (Dea Mater).[59]

M. von Heland, in an ample analysis of the patera from Petroasa,[60] put forward a somewhat similar hypothesis. According to the Swedish researcher, the figured frieze of the patera from Pietroasa could derive from different mystery cults based on the "mother Goddess" and possibly associated with the cult of Sabazios, which is closely connected with that of the Mother Goddess, Sabazios being her son and husband at the same time.[61] On the basis of stylistic analysis of the patera from Pietroasa, von Heland discerns some elements of the Gandhara style in the contrast between the rigidity of the central figures and the dynamism of the figures which flank them, Sassanian elements in some details of clothing, and especially Parthian influences in the proportions of the body and the facial shapes, or Hellenistic in the manner of representation of the human body.

According to the view of von Heland, the close relation between the patera and the repertory of Parthian art and the artistic syncretism which is attested by the style are arguments in favour of locating the centre of production in Syria, more exactly at Antioch[62] and as regards the chronology, a date around 360, probably 363, has been proposed. The piece has been interpreted as a magnificent gift given to the temple of Cybele which was reconstructed by Julian.[63]

The hypothesis that the piece was manufactured in the capital of Syria seems to me very plausible; Antioch, with its splendid squares, with its streets 36 stadii (6.5 km) in length, with its baths and lights, and with its mixed population which was more pagan than Christian, remained "the pearl of the Orient",[64] even after the foundation of Constantinople. The date proposed by von Heland, around 360 and certainly no later, can be accepted in all probability.

There is no direct information as to the way in which the patera arrived at Pietroasa. However, taking into consideration the Hunnic expedition of 395,[65] when the Huns reach Antioch. we can put forward the hypothesis that the patera fell into the hands of the Huns or of some allied people at that time and then the patera, together with other items, arrived in the Carpathian region with the movement of the large mass of Huns to the West.

In conclusion, we believe that the patera was manufactured in Antioch in around A.D. 360 and must be associated with the attempt of Julian to restore the pagan religion;[66] the presence of this object in Romania must be connected with the migration of the mixed ethnic mass led by the Huns to the West. For other more precise details there is no documentary evidence.

Multiangular cups (Pl. VII-VIII)

a) Octagonal cup (Pl. VII). The cup is 10.5 cm in height. The sides consist of two rows of eight pierced panels each overlapping each other on different planes; one is vertical, the other is oblique and both are joined with a narrow pierced frame. The base, with eight sides, is flat and has a small frame. The two handles are modelled in the shape of panthers with the back legs on the edge of the cup and the front legs on the edge of a horizontal plate cut in the shape of a bird's tail; the handles are attached to the lip of the cup by rivets.

The two rows of panels representing the sides of the cup consist of rosettes with eight to twelve petals set with garnets; the free space between them was filled with rock-crystal. Even the frames which join the panels are decorated with rows of rectangles filled with garnets. The lip of the cup and the edge of the base are doubled (for solidity) with gold bands. The horizontal plates which form the upper part of the handles were decorated with a net of rosettes filled with garnets. A small garnet engraved with concentric circles preserved in its original place shows that the stones were flat.

b) Twelve-sided cup (Pl. VIII). Height 11 cm. Two rows of 12 panels overlap each other, one horizontal, the other oblique. The panels are more elongated than those of the octagonal cup, the rosettes arranged in their centres are smaller and more massive and the space around them is larger. Vertical strips join the rosettes with the edges of the panels. The base, preserved in its entirety, is decorated with a rosette inscribed in a circle.

We will deal with the other decorative details when we consider the polychrome style.

The differences between these two pieces are not very important for the present analysis. Both cups present similar features in the multi-angular form, the polychrome style and the handles in the shape of panthers.

It has been suggested that, according to the form of the cups, analogies could be drawn with some types of metal vessels from the Roman period. Vessels from the treasures found at Boscoreale and Hildesheim dating from the first century A.D. or from the hoard discovered at Ostriovany in Slovakia (third century A.D.) have been considered as arguments in support of this analogy.[67] However, this is more a formal than a real analogy and for this reason it is irrelevant.

Furthermore, study of the shape of the handles cannot help us very much. Such handles, modelled particularly in the shape of felines, are also encountered on Graeco-Roman metal vessels from the first centuries A.D.,[68] or on one of the pendants from the treasure no. 1 found at Simleul Silvaniei[69] (Fig. 2:2). The panther pattern lasts for a long time, as it is very convincingly attested by a bracelet consisting of two panthers, coming probably from Egypt and dating from the 7th century A.D.;[70] it imitated Byzantine jewellery from the 5th century A.D.

Closer analogies can be drawn and more precise dating can be determined only on the basis of the polychrome style in which the cups are worked, and this we will discuss further.

Before ending the discussion of the "sacred" vessels from the Pietroasa treasure we should mention the conclusion formulated by K. Horedt; according to him late antique vessels of precious metal occur in princely tombs in the 5th century,[71] and in general, this practice is typical of the Hunnic period.[72] In my opinion the hoard found at Tăutenu-Bihor[73] in 1970 must be judged in this context.

The personal ornaments from the Pietroasa treasure belong to two distinct categories, ornaments worn round the neck (three collars) and fibulae. From the stylistic point of view, we can distinguish two groups, namely pieces made of massive gold (the plain collar and the inscribed collar) and the pieces worked in polychrome style (the hinged collar and the fibulae).

The plain collar (Pl. IX:1, diameter 17 cm) is made of a massive gold band which is round in section (diameter 0.5 cm) with a loop and hook for fastening. The loop results from the bending and the flattening of one of the terminals and the hook from the bending of the opposite terminal (Ösenhalsring).

This ornament is typical of the graves of men of the period of Attila and reflects a fashion which was widespread in over a large area from Western Sibera to Central Europe.[74]

It should be noted that the collar with hook and loop for fastening also occurs sporadically in the 4th century A.D., as is attested by the bronze collar from Piatra Frecăței[75] or the silver one found at Novi Banovici.[76] However, gold examples occur only in the 5th century A.D. or certainly not earlier than the end of the 4th century A.D., as seems to be indicated by the grave with collar, silver plated bronze fibula and jug with burnished decoration from Budapest X, Keresztuvi, of which we still do not have more precise information.[77]

This assertion is based on finds from closed complexes.[78] For example, a collar of this type has been found in the grave from Musliumova, Perm (Fig. 4:1-2), together with buckles worked in polychrome style typical of the 5th century and with a harnass-ring typical to the Untersiebenbrunn-Coşovenii de Jos horizon which dates the tomb to the beginning of the 5th century (Fig. 4:1).[79] On the basis of the grave-goods which also include a collar of this type, the princely tomb from Szeged-Nagyszekso (Fig. 5:1-2) is dated to between 420 and 430.[80]

In the grave from Keszthely, the collar was associated with oval buckles with rectangular plates, typical of the first half of the 5th century.[81]

The analogy between the plain collar and the collar belonging to the princely grave found at Untersebenbrunn[82] is of great importance for the dating of the Pietroasa treasure. We will give details of this analogy in the section of the present study dealing with the relation between the pieces or rather between the styles of the Pietroasa treasure and the Untersiebenbrunn-Coşovenii de Jos cultural groups. Another analogy with the plain collar exists in the princely grave from Pouan (Fig. 6:1); on the basis of the polychrome style in which the weapons (Spatha and Scramasax) and some buckles are worked, the tomb is dated to around 450.[83]

In conclusion, all the collars of massive gold, with loop and hook for fastening and which have been found in closed complexes are dated within the 5th century, especially in the first half of that century and consequently this dating must also be admitted for the collar from Pietroasa.

The collar with inscription (Pl. IX:2)

The piece is made of a band which is thicker (1.2 cm) in the middle and thinner at the terminals. The terminals, strengthened by a wire twisted 15-16 times in spirals, has loop and hook for fastening in the same manner as the plain collar. The inscription, in German runes, is engraved on the middle of the collar on the outer side.

Various interpretations have been given for this piece; it has been considered as a bracelet, dog collar, ritual ring belonging to the door of a temple, or even as a ring for a wine jug. On the basis of analogies with the plain collar and consequently with other pieces of the same kind, there is no doubt that this piece was also an ornament worn round the neck, namely, a collar or torque.

The inscription engraved on it has also been variously interpreted.[84] Taking into account the primary object of our study, we cannot dwell on the details of the problem of the inscription, which can be solved only on the basis of philological study. The reading proposed by Neumeister (among numerous other hypotheses) in 1868,[85] seems to be the most plausible. R. Neumeister read gutaniowi hailag and proposed three variant translations: a) "to Wodan, sacred"; b) "to the good country of the Scythians, sacred"; c) "to the good fatherland, sacred". M. Isbăşescu[86] proposed gutani o wi hailag or gutanio wi hailag, translated "hereditary sacrosanct master (or protector) of the Gothi". Several scholars agree with the suggestion put forward by R. Loewe in 1910: gutan Iowi hailag, in translation "to Jupiter of the Gothi, devoted".[89]

Regardless of the future solution of this problem, in the present stage of research we can assert that the piece under discussion is a torque reflecting a certain social position and the inscription, probably engraved in a later period,[88] is in the runic alphabet and attests that the treasure belonged to a Gothic tribe.[89]

Torques of this type are depicted frequently on different objects dating from the second half of the 4th century or the beginning of the 5th century and they are confined to a restricted circle, namely the members of the imperial guard. For example, we would cite in support of this view the diptych from Halberstadt dating from the beginning of the 5th century or the missorium of Theodosius I from A.D. 388 (Museum of Madrid, Real Academia de la Historia),[90] where the members of the imperial guard wear similar ornaments round their neck.

There is also some information in the literary sources which refer to such objects. On the occasion of the murder of a group of barbarians, probably Goths, in the Dobrudja in 388, Gerontius, the perpetrator of the massacre, captured the gifts given by the emperor to the barbarians "which consisted of gold collars given by the emperor to them for their adornment" (Zosimus, IV, 40, 20).

The collar with hinge (Pl. X). So far as I know there are few analogies with this piece in the 3rd-6th centuries.

The collar is of eliptical form and consists of two unequal parts (diameter 20 and 15 cm) joined with hinges. The largest and broadest part, sloping in the shape of a truncated cone, is suitable to enclose the neck. The piece is made of two overlapping gold plates soldered at the edges. The front plate is thin and pierced and the back plate is thick and plain. The piece was decorated by cutting a net of recesses in varied shapes, the pattern consisting of overlapping hearts and stylized flowers and leaves are predominant. A resinous substance was applied between the pierced plate and the base plate to make it solid. The two hinges of the collar have as a pin a piece of wire with a garnet on the upper part.

The form of this ornament is known both in Scandinavia and Germany in the Bronze Age [91] and in the Scythian culture from the middle of the first millennium B.C.[92] But these specimens cannot be considered as prototypes; on the basis of our present documentary evidence we cannot determine the development of this piece. An object, interpreted as a triumphal crown, represented on the mosaic of the apse dome of the church of San Vitale, Ravenna[93] dating from the 6th century, can be considered as an approximate, though not identical, analogy which supports the later dating. The polychrome style in which the collar is worked indicates, as we will show later, the first half of the 5th century.

The small (Pl. XI) and middle size (Pl. XII) fibulae consist of three distinct parts, a disc-shaped central part, the lyre-shaped plate at the terminal of the fibula, and the foot in the shape of a stylized bird. Both the head and the foot are soldered to the middle part. The catch-system is soldered to the back of the head-plate and is identical with that of the "crossbow" fibulae (Zwiebelknopffibel) from the late Roman and Roman-Byzantine period.

The small fibula (Pl. XI), is 12.5 cm high, without the chains. Two rectangular plates with four recesses each, filled with rock-crystal, are attached to both sides of the body. Two plates cut in the shape of wings and ending in spirals are attached to the lateral sides of the lower plate. A round garnet is placed on each plate. Chains with ovoidal pendants hang from two rings attached to the back of the lower plate. The spring, borrowed from the "crossbow" fibulae, is also attached to this plate, The rectangular plate on the opposite side is flanked by two round garnets; the upper part is decorated with trapezoidal square and hexagonal recesses. These overlapping geometrical figures are separated from each other by a granulated gold wire with granules at the ends. A pyramid-shaped tube backs the upper part of the fibula. The six-sided base of the tube is provided with a recess set with a garnet.

The small fibula from Pietroasa results from the fusion of two types of fibulae; the oval central part derives from the late Roman oval fibula with dish and the catching system is borrowed from the "crossbow" fibula mentioned above. The highly stylized bird-head of the small fibula is of Oriental influence.[94]

These typological affinities with the fibulae from the Simleul Silvaniei hoard are of special importance for the chronology of the Pietroasa treasure. The fibulae with semi-disc and elongated foot are very important for the dating of the Simleul Silvaniei hoard. Identical or almost identical analogies with the fibulae with semi-disc and elongated foot from the second hoard of Simleul Silvaniei[97] exist at Kerch, where similar fibulae have been found together with coins in graves; on the basis of the fact that these coins are issues of Valentinian I (364-375) and Valentinian II (375-392) this type of fibula is dated in the South of the USSR to the end of the 4th century.[98] As regards the fibulae of the same type discovered at Airan,[99] Untersiebenbrunn[100] (Fig. 13:1-2) and Simleul Silvaniei (Fig. 2) they should be dated in the first half of the 5th century[101] and consequently the small fibula and also the middle size fibulae, as we will show further, found at Pietroasa, might be dated in the same period. The dating of the Simleul Silvaniei treasure to the first half of the 5th century on the basis of the date assigned to these fibulae could be available for all the pieces composing the hoard, including also the fibula with onyx. Since it is a hoard, it is composed of pieces from different periods, but still in circulation at the date when the treasure was hidden.

The study of the catch-system which was borrowed from the "crossbow" fibula, can date more precisely the small fibula from Pietroasa. Close analogies can be drawn between the knobs of the small fibula found at Pietroasa and type 6 of the classification of this kind of ornament established by E. Keller.[102] On the other hand, the knobs of the fibula with onyx from Simleul Silvaniei are analogous with the knobs of type 5 in the typology of Keller.[103] Bearing in mind that, on the basis of the coin-finds, type 5 is dated between 370 and 400 and type 6 dates from the beginning of the 5th century,[104] we must admit that the small fibula from Pietroasa dates from the first half of the 5th century, towards the beginning of the century. This slight chronological difference between the fibula with onyx from Simleul Silvaniei and the small fibula from Pietroasa, is an argument in favour of the hypothesis put forward by Fettich with regard to the development-stages of this type of fibula.

The observations concerning the typological development of the small fibula also apply in the case of the middle size fibulae (Pl. XII); they represent the last typological phase within the typology proposed by Fettich.

The fibulae are 25 cm in height (without chains). The ovoid body is made of two overlapping convex plates which are soldered on the edge. One of the plates is the front of the fibula and the other is the back. The front is set with rows of <u>flat</u> garnets, in the shape of leaves, hearts and circles enclosing the large oval and bulged stone placed in the centre. Concentric circles were engraved on all the flat stones.

The thin and curved neck (to the back) of the birds consists of a row of oval and round recesses, which were probably filled with garnets, separated from each other by a granulated wire. Recesses with small stones and small vertical tubes with a gold granule set on the top, completed the edge of the neck. A plate in the shape of a base of a lyre is attached to the lower edge of the ovoidal body and covers the spring of the fibula and is also borrowed from the "crossbow" fibula where it is attached to its back. Five large <u>cabochon</u> and recesses filled with flat garnets exist on the surface of this plate. Twisted chains hang down from three small rings and end, by forking, with five gold granules enclosed in settings engraved with imbrications and set with flat stones.

The observations concerning the knobs of the catch-system of the small fibula also apply to the knobs of the middle size fibulae and for this reason the dating proposed for the small fibula should also be admitted for the middle size fibulae. On the other hand, the long neck with bird-head of the middle size fibulae is encountered on the cup from Gourdon dating to about 450[105] and in my opinion this is an argument which supports the dating of the middle size fibula in the first half of the 5th century.

One of the major questions posed by both the middle size and the large fibulae is caused by the adoption of the eagle design which appears on the three fibulae and on the oenochoe-jug.[106]

This motif occurs on numerous objects such as buckles, weapons, pieces of harness, collars, fibulae, pottery, appliqués etc. dating from the 5th-6th centuries A.D.[107] The problem concerns the cultural area whence the Goths adopted this pattern, and which was diffused through the whole of Europe by their agency.

The eagle-motif is widespread in Scythian art to the North of the Black Sea from the end of the 7th century and the beginning of the 6th century B.C. This is attested by the following finds: pieces of harness found in the barrow from Kelermes (the region of Krasnodar),[108] the ornamental piece discovered in barrow 2 from Ulskii Aul (Kuban),[109] 17 eagles at Melgunov (the region of Kirovograd),[110] buckle-plaque from Zolotoi-Kurgan (Crimea)[111] approximating to the form of the large fibula, and bronze pieces of harness found in barrow 24 from Nimgei (Crimea).[112] This pattern spread from this area to the different cultures of the population of the Altai, where it occurs in a more naturalistic style than in Scythian art. We cite as examples the ornamental plaque from harness discovered in barrow 1 from Tuetka,[113] the ornamental plaque discovered in the barrow from Beşadar[114] and the piece of harness from barrow 3 at Pazyryk.[115]

The pattern, which according to some authors came from Asia Minor,[116] lasted for a long time in these regions. It is encountered in Sarmatian art from the 2nd-3rd centuries A.D., for example in the diadem from Novocherkask or the tree with birds (<u>Vogelbaum</u>) from barrow 46 at Ust-Labinskaia, near Krasnodar.[117]

On the other hand, this pattern is encountered on several belt-ornaments in China from the period of the Han dynasty[118] (202 B.C.-A.D. 220), whose military action eventually caused the migration of some Hunnic tribes to the West.

Contact with the Chinese civilisation of the Han dynasty and with the cultures of the Altai population, in addition to the influence exerted by the Sarmatian culture of the North of the Black Sea in the final period brought about the definitive adoption of this motif by the Hunnic tribes. Among the animal motifs which were frequent in these cultural areas, only this one was adopted by the Huns and consequently it gained a considerable importance.[119]

As regards the adoption of this pattern by the German tribes, namely the Goths, we consider that the eagle pattern could penetrate into the Gothic cultural and spiritual milieu only after the Gothic tribes to the North of the Black Sea were included in the Hunnic confederation and we believe that its adoption must be considered as a recognition of Hunnic supremacy. There is no evidence within the Sîntana de Mureş-Cerneahov culture to support the hypothesis that this motif was adopted from the Sarmatian milieu, as J. Werner inclined to consider the "eagles" from Pietroasa.[120]

This motif is widespread at the end of the 4th century and the beginning of the next century. Besides the objects reflecting a certain social position within Hunnic society, the eagle appears also on more modest pieces, as for example the flagon of Sîntana de Mureş-Cerneahov tradition, discovered at Regöly and mentioned above.

The large fibula (Pl. XIII)

The height of this piece without the chains is 27 cm, the width at the breast 15 cm. The body of the fibula is similar to that of a bird, and is made of a thick gold plate which is a little bent to permit the placing of the ornament on the shoulder. The tubular worked neck and head were soldered on this plate; recesses filled with stones were also soldered on the same plate. Eight chains (four above and four below) attached to the back of the plate, and were used for the catching of the chains twisted in thin gold wire, each ending with a box-setting with an ovoid granule of rock-crystal.

The round neck of the bird is decorated with parallel rows of hearts set with flat garnets and small dimples filled with small round stones are placed below the eyes, represented by two oval shaped garnets. The representation of the head seems to be more natural, in contrast with the very stylized body.

A rectangular thinner plate was soldered on the back of the plate representing the body of the bird to strengthen the central stone set on the front. The part which supported the spring of the fibula, at present lost, was strengthened in the same manner. A device with facets vertically placed supports the foot (in the shape of a lateral open sheet) of the fibula. Thin granulated wire covered all the solderings.

The large fibula is without parallels. Possibly it served as a prototype for the eagle-shaped fibulae from Ostrogothic Italy or Visigothic Spain, in spite of the fact that the typological intermediary links are lacking for the moment.[121]

The fibula was worn on the shoulder as is attested by the bend of the piece, the rings for the pendants placed at both ends of the plate of the fibula and the pierced neck of the eagle.[122] On the basis of the fact that the fibula was worn on the shoulder and not on the breast of the bearer, D. Brown proposed a new restoration of this piece according to which the head must be turned sideways through 180°.[123] According to him, the middle size fibulae were worn on the breast,[124] and he also thinks that the large fibula was a clothing accessory for a man's garment while the middle size fibulae were accessories of a woman's dress.[125]

The ovoid body of the fibulae from Pietroasa, the setting with precious stones and the chains with pendants indicate a type of fibula which was worn only by the imperial family.[126] This type occurs for the first time on a silver dish from the Kerch treasure (Hospital Street) which contained, among other items, an oenochoe-jug which is analogous with that belonging to the Pietroasa treasure.[127] This dish, which on the basis of the inscription is dated to 343, is decorated with the bust of Constantius II wearing a fibula with a round plate with pendants on the shoulder.[128] This is a very plain type of fibula which might have served at most as a prototype to the fibulae typical of the imperial garment from the end of the 4th century.

Fibulae with more complicated pendants[129] which can be associated with the fibulae from Pietroasa occur only from the period of Valens; they are encountered on medallions, coins or on other objects of marble or ivory.

For example a fibula which has close analogies with the small fibula from Pietroasa appears on the large medallion of the emperor Valens exhibited in the Kunsthistoriches Museum in Vienna. Another parallel can be drawn between the small fibula from the Pietroasa treasure and the dyptich representing Rome and Constantinople and dating from the beginning of the 5th century[131] (Fig. 7:2), belonging to the same museum.

The small fibula from Pietroasa has close analogies with the fibula encountered on the bronze bust from the Hungarian National Museum in Budapest; it is attributed to Valentinian II,[132] and not to Constans I[133] and is dated to about 388[134] (Fig. 7:3). This new fashion is widespread during the following centuries and according to N. Beleaev lasted until the 10th century.[135]

The consular dyptich from the treasure of Halberstadt cathedral and dating from the beginning of the 5th century (Fig. 7:1) is of great importance for the problems of the Pietroasa treasure.[136] The tablets of the dyptich are divided in three zones. The upper zone is decorated with the figures of two emperors, the image of Rome on the left and Constantinople on the right side. The two emperors wear chlamys and wear a fibula on the shoulder; this fibula is analogous with the middle size fibulae from Pietroasa.

All these analogies, dating from the end of the 4th century and the beginning of the next century, support the above-proposed dating of the fibulae from Pietroasa. At the same time the fibulae from Pietroasa represent an imitation of the imperial fashion which becomes dominant towards the end of the 4th century and at the beginning of the next century.[137]

CHAPTER 3

THE POLYCHROME STYLE OF THE PIETROASA TREASURE
AND OF OTHER FINDS FROM THE TERRITORY OF ROMANIA

The polychrome style is a decorative technique and consists of encrusting vessels and ornaments of gold with precious and semi-precious stones and sometimes with glass. The revival of the ancient Persian polychrome art in the milieu of the Iranian-Sarmatians situated to the North of the Black Sea during the last centuries B.C., brought about the diffusion of the polychrome style over a large geographical area, from Siberia to Syria, Greece and Italy. The polychrome style spread, both by the intermediary of the Goths and directly, through the Mediterranean basin over the whole of Europe in the 4th-6th centuries. There are three main techniques of encrusting with precious stones: a) <u>en cabochon,</u> where the stones are set in the independent recesses; b) <u>cloisonné,</u> where the ornamental stones are set in a network of recesses soldered on the gold plate; c) <u>à jour:</u> the recess for stones is cut in the plate of precious metal, sometimes the recess being transparent.[138]

All the red stones which decorate the Pietroasa treasure are garnets;[139] these precious stones are largely found in Asia Minor and to the North of the Black Sea. Besides them, a green stone, spinel, was also used, for example on the collar with hinge or on the multiangular cups.[140] From the point of view of the technique of cutting stones, three categories of ornamental stones can be distinguished within the Pietroasa treasure. The first category consists of the bulged garnets on the large and middle-size fibulae. A narrow slit is cut into the stone with a point of diamond, and after this operation the stone is broken and polished. Sometimes, for example in the case of the middle-size fibulae, the garnets are decorated with concentric circles which have been engraved with a very sharp diamond point (Pl. XII). The second category comprises the flat garnets cut with a small wheel and which appear on the collar with hinge, the multiangular cups and the small fibula but also on the middle-size fibulae or on the large one (Pl. VII-VIII; X-XIII). The third category includes the garnets similar to fluted sticks, for example in the decoration on the handles of the multiangular cups (Pl. VII:2; VIII:2).

The flat garnets occur in three shapes namely, garnets in the shape of hearts (the collar with hinge, the three fibulae - Pl. X; XI-XIII), palmettes (the collar with hinge, the multiangular cups - Pl. VII-VIII; X), and acanthus-leaves (the collar with hinge, the large fibula, the multiangular cups - Pl. VII-VIII; X; XII). The maximum thickness of the garnets from Pietroasa is 1.3 mm. According to B. Arrhenius[141] the thickness of the garnets could provide dating evidence, for the thicker garnets are earlier and the thinner ones later. If we consider that the garnets from Pietroasa are thinner than those found in Childeric's tomb at Tournay or than the garnets on the cup with

19

pedestal from Goudron,[142] dating to the second half or the middle of the 5th century, then in my opinion this would be another argument in support of the hypothesis that the pieces encrusted with such garnets from the Pietroasa treasure date from the 5th century.

In the Pietroasa treasure, all three setting techniques have been used for encrusting the garnets.

The large and middle-size fibulae are worked in the cabochon technique (Pl. XII-XIII). The stone is fixed in an independent recess soldered on the metal support, backed by a cement composition consisting of charcoal and other substances.

The cloisonné technique was used for the decoration of the handles of the multiangular baskets and of the large fibula (Pl. VII-VIII; XIII). The cement is the same as in the case of the cabochon technique.

The third technique of setting stones typical of the polychrome style is the technique à jour. The neck of the large fibula (Pl. XIII), the multiangular cups (Pl. VII-VIII), the small fibula (Pl. XI) and the middle size fibulae (Pl. XII) and the collar with hinge (Pl. X) are worked in this type of technique.

The stone is translucent in the case of the large fibula (Pl. XIII) and the multiangular cups (Pl. VII-VIII) while the collar with hinge (Pl. X), the small fibula (Pl. XI) and the middle size fibulae (Pl. XII) have the pierced plate in which the stones were encrusted fixed on a metal support. The cement composition consisting of organic substances filled the space between these two plates.

An interesting variant of this technique is encountered in the handles of the multiangular baskets (Pl. VII-VIII). The bulged garnets are set into recesses cut in the shape of the precious stones in the gold plate. The top edge of these recesses were turned over to keep the ornamental stone in place. An inside plate in the shape of the outside plate backed the stones.

On the basis of the analysis of the objects worked in the polychrome style which have been found in Romania (Fig. 8, (see Appendix 1), we can distinguish several stylistic groups (Fig. 9). The first group comprises the pieces decorated exclusively with cabochon work. The majority of this group consist of diadems or fragments of diadems, which is the typical ornament of the nomadic Huns and dates from the end of the 4th century and the beginning of the 5th century.[143] The finds from Buhăeni, Dulceanca, Gherăseni, and Bălteni belong to this category. The cabochon technique is typical of the fibula from Chiojd which was discovered in a grave dating from the first half of the 5th century[144] or of the fragment of pendant discovered at Rotopănești and also dating from the first half of the 5th century.[145] According to the objects worked exclusively in this technique which have been found in Romania, the polychrome style en cabochon belongs to the end of the 4th century and the beginning of the next century.

Another group consists of the objects worked in the cloisonné technique and belonging to the same period, ear-rings with polyhedron cube (Hunedoara, Mediaș, Izvin) and shoe-buckles (Cîlnău, Brașov). The shoe-buckles from Brașov and Cîlnău belong to a category of buckles which is typical of the period of Attila; taking into account the position in which the buckles of this type have been placed in the graves at Jakuszowice and at Laa-an-der-Yhaye, (tomb 2), the buckles of Brașov and Cîlnău belonged to shoes. These buckles are typical of the first half of the 5th century and are encountered in a very large area from Southern Russia to North Africa which suggests that they were products of late workshops.[146]

This chronology is confirmed by finds in which the two techniques are associated. The third group is encountered either in graves (Vețel, Periam) or in princely tombs or hoards (Concești and Simleul Silvaniei).

The tomb at Vețel containing an ear-ring with polyhedron cube and a fibula with semi-circular plate and elongated foot similar to those from the Simleul Silvaniei hoard (Fig. 2:1) belongs, as we have mentioned, to the end of the 4th century and the first half of the 5th century.[147]

The tomb at Periam, which contained two silver fibulae with the lateral frames decorated in cloisonné technique is dated, on the basis of the fibulae with disc with undecorated broad frames and elongated foot, (variant III - K. Horedt, dating after 450)[148] in the second half of the 5th century. The relatively modest feature of the find explains the absence of other decorative techniques.

Finally, the last representative of this group, the tomb at Concesti, in which the cloisonnée technique appears on the appliqué in the shape of an eagle and on the plaques from harness and the cabochon technique occurs on other plaques and on the triangular appliqué,[150] is dated, according to the analysis of its component pieces, to the first decades of the 5th century.[151]

In contrast to the tombs of Vețel and Periam, whose relatively modest grave-goods justifies the absence of other decorative techniques, the princely tomb of Concești or the hoard of Simleul Silvaniei are finds of considerable richness and we believe that the absence of some decorative techniques of the polychrome style is of chronological significance.

In my opinion this is attested by the fourth group of the polychrome style in Romania which is represented by the Pietroasa treasure, the princely graves from Apahida and the Someșeni hoard.

The stylistic link between the four archaeological finds is attested, besides by the presence of the cabochon technique (Pietroasa - Pl. XII-XIII, Apahida I,[152] Someșeni)[153] or of the cloisonné technique in straight <u>cloisons</u> (Pietroasa - ex. Pl. VII-VIII, Apahida I - Fig. 10:4-8,[154] Apahida II Fig. 11:3,[155] Someșeni Fig. 12:3)[156] also by the presence of pierced cloisonné both at Pietrosa and Someșeni (Fig. 12:1-2)[157] and by the use of garnets in the shape of fluted sticks at Pietroasa, Aphida I (Fig. 10:3-3)[158] and Apahida II (Fig. 11:1-4).[159]

The garnets in the shape of hearts on the collar from Pietroasa appear also on the lion-shaped fibula from Simleul Silvaniei (Fig. 3:2) and on the sheath of the sword (<u>Spatha</u>) found in grave 2 at Apahida.[160]

The dating of this group is based on the finds from Apahida and Someșeni. Grave 1 at Apahida is dated by analogies to the second half of the 5th century ($\pm$ 480)[161] and the hoard from Cluj-Someșeni belongs to the same periods.[162]

A date before the middle of the 5th century is proposed for tomb 2 from Apahida.[163] In my opinion the close stylistic link between the two princely tombs of Apahida, which is shown by the presence of the wavy cloisonné and especially by the existence of other variants of cloisonné [164] which do not occur at Pietroasa allow us to also date tomb 2 at Apahida to the second half of the 5th century.

In these circumstances, and taking into account the links existing between the finds under discussion, the dating of the Pietroasa treasure to the first half of the 5th century is supported by real evidence. The chronological difference results basically from the presence of the wavy cloisonné associated with the umbo-shaped cloisonnee (mit halbkreisförmiger Ausbuchtung) in both tombs of Apahida, and which are dated by J. Werner, on the basis of the parade-buckles found at Köln-Severinstor, to the second half of the 5th century.[165]

CHAPTER 4

LINKS WITH OTHER CULTURAL GROUPS

The dating and the cultural attribution of the Pietroasa treasure can also be established by relating the typological and cultural contents of this hoard to other neighbouring cultural groups. Comparison can be made with two cultures, the Sîntana de Mureş-Cerneahov culture of the 4th century A.D. and the Unterseibenbrunn-Coşovenii de Jos culture of the first half of the 5th century A.D.

a) <u>Links with the Sîntana de Mureş-Cerneahov culture</u>

The Sîntana de Mureş-Cerneahov culture is characterised by the large biritual cemeteries, in which inhumation-burials orientated North-South are predominant, and the unfortified settlements with sunken-floored huts and surface-dwellings. The graves contain relatively rich grave-goods, consisting of silver or bronze fibulae, combs, plain buckles, pottery etc. Swords[166] and gold objects are lacking, at least in the complexes belonging to the variant which is typical of Romania. The Sîntana de Mureş-Cerneahov culture is dated from the end of the 3rd century to the end of the 4th century.

This culture is a synthesis of several ethnic elements; according to the ritual practices and the grave-goods, the following components have been noted: Gotho-Sarmatian, Taifalic (the Tîrgşor-Olteni aspect) and native Dacian (the Tîrgşor-Gheraseni aspect).[167]

From the point of view of the burial rite and ritual, we can distinguish a clear-cut difference between the cemeteries of the Sîntana de Mureş-Cerneahov culture and those with finds worked in the polychrome style. All the finds which are characterized by the polychrome style did not occur in the large cemeteries but are isolated finds and this is explained by the special social position of the wearers of ornaments decorated in the polychrome style.

We do not know of graves with artificially deformed skulls, such as those discovered in the graves with diadems at Buhăeni or Gherăseni. On the other hand deformed skulls occur also in larger cemeteries typical of the first half of the 5th century and in which the polychrome style is absent, as, for example, the necropolis of Botoşani-Dealu Cărămidăriei,[168] where the deformed skulls are associated with other eastern elements which are characteristic of the finds of the polychrome style. We refer primarily to the mirrors of the Omi Brigetio type in grave 8[169] which have a perfect analogy in the princely tomb discovered at Untersiebenbrunn.[170] Consequently, as regards the first half of the 5th century, we can establish a link between the rich finds characterized by the polychrome style and the more modest finds in the cemeteries where this style is absent. This connection has not been established in the case of the Sîntana de Mureş culture.

This situation is explained by the fact that the Sîntana de Mureş-Cerneahov culture is a rural one with few Eastern infiltrations during the 4th century, but with evident Roman influences. After the disappearance of the classic form of the Sîntana de Mureş-Cerneahov culture, as a result of the Visigoths crossing into the Empire, traces of the indigenous population continue to appear to the North of the Danube in the 5th century as is archaeologically attested at Ciresanu[172] or Costişa-Mănoaia-Botoşana.[173] But the two cultural horizons do not exclude each other completely and this is demonstrated by the iron fibulae plated with a gold sheet and encrusted with stones on the head and foot which have been discovered at Izvoru, district of Ilfov.[174] But it is a rudimentary technique and the grave belongs in all probability to the last phase of the culture.

The decoration consisting of concentric circles on some middle size or small fibulae (Pl. XI:1, XII:2) lead to the same conclusion. This decoration, which is probably of Roman origin, appears on several objects typical of the Sîntana de Mureş-Cerneahov culture (combs, pendants etc.) but continues to be used after the end of this culture, as is suggested by the comb found in the grave at Lebeny dating from the first half of the 5th century.[175]

The persistence of some traditions of the Sîntana de Mureş-Cerneahov culture after it ceased in its classic forms is also attested in other geographical areas. For example, ornaments worked in the polychrome style have been found together with pottery of the Sîntana de Mureş tradition in the settlement at Bela Nikopolja situated in the forest steppe to the North of the Black Sea.[176]

The same fact is attested by the grave-goods of tomb 11 at Inkerman (Crimea); silver fibulae are associated with nomadic mirrors typical of the 5th century.[177]

These archaeological finds suggest that the most advanced elements of the Cerneahov culture penetrated to the South and brought about a cultural synthesis in the regions situated to the North of the Black Sea. The conquest of these regions by the Huns gave an impetus to this synthesis, containing Sarmatian and Bosporan elements. Certainly, this process was accompanied by important social changes, whose archaeological echo is the great princely graves and hoards from the end of the 4th century and the beginning of the 5th century.[178]

On the other hand, we must take into account also another very significant circumstance which can explain the appearance of the princely graves. It seems that contact between a human community which was stratified from a social point of view and a superior civilization (Hochkulturen) was also a cause which brought about this phenomenon. There is an internal tendency of the ruling class of these communities to show, by garment and pompous burial ritual, as is suggested by the archaeological situation in the 5th century, their special social position as the superior partner.[179]

The Sîntana de Mureş-Cerneahov tradition continues to persist in some regions of the Carpathian basin in the second half of the 5th century. This is well attested in Hungary by the pottery found in the graves at Regöly[180] or Lebeny,[181] in contrast with Transylvania where the situation is not very clear.[182] According to the most recent opinion, in Hungary we can refer solely to the persistence of some tradition and in no case to the effective presence of this culture at the end of the 4th century and the beginning of the following century.[183] This situation is confirmed in Moravia by the grave at Smolin[184] and even in Bavaria by the grave at Götting.[185]

This summary survey of the relations between the polychrome groups and the Sîntana de Mureș-Cerneahov culture lead to the conclusion that during the development of the polychrome style, whose magnificence is represented in the Pietroasa treasure, we can identify the continuation of only some Cerneahov traditions.

In these circumstances, the attribution of the Pietroasa treasure to Athanaric, whose supremacy coincides with the period of the maximum development of the Sîntana de Mureș-Cerneahov culture, can hardly be supported by the archaeological evidence.

b) <u>Links with the Untersiebenbrunn-Coșovenii de Jos culture</u>

One of the characteristic elements of this cultural horizon consists of the different categories of metal antiquities, especially of silver, such as pieces of harness, bridles, harness-rings, and pendants, or belt-fittings with engraved decoration, which occur both in hoards and princely tombs discovered over a very large area from Sweden to the Lower Danube and from the Bug to Western Europe.[186]

The relation between this positive industry of metal decorated by engraving and the polychrome style is attested by several finds from closed complexes. For example, pendants of the type found at Coșovenii de Jos (Fig. 1:2,6) or at Untersiebenbrunn (Fig. 14:1-2)[188] decorated in this technique occur together with fibulae worked in polychrome style (Fig. 13:1-2)[189] in the deposit of Laskov (Volhinia). The same association between the polychrome style and engraved decoration is encountered in the princely tomb discovered at Jakuszowice (Fig. 15:22-28), where pieces of harness of belt-fittings appear together with <u>cloisonné</u> shoe buckles of the same type as those found at Brașov or at Posta Cîlnăului, or with ornamental pieces decorated with <u>cabochon</u>.[190] The two techniques are associated on the same object, in the case of the collar from Eskjö (Smaland-Sweden).[191] The most typical example of this is perhaps the princely grave found at Untersiebenbrunn (Fig. 13, 14).[192]

All these associations demonstrate that the polychrome style during a certain phase of its development was contemporary with this cultural horizon.

As regards the Pietroasa treasure there are multiple links with finds typical of the Untersiebenbrunn-Coșovenii de Jos cultural horizon. As we have mentioned, both the neck and the foot of the oenochoe-jug (Pl. II) have engraved decoration worked in a technique which is typical of this culture.

Even the motif of stylized acanthus leaves is encountered on the chain with pendants from hoard 1 found at Simleul Silvaniei (Fig. 2:2),[194] and this fact is a new argument in support of a close connection with hoard 2.[195]

On the other hand acanthus-leaves, worked in the cloisonné style, occur also on the handles of the multiangular cups (Pl. VIII).[196] This very close stylistic connection shows that the two pieces under discussion were contemporaneous. The heart-shaped cloisonné motif on a harness-ring of the Untersiebenbrunn-Coşovenii de Jos culture which has been discovered at Kerch (Fig. 1:9) and is closely related to the cloisonné decoration of the pectoral ornament from Pietroasa lead to the same conclusion.[197]

All these facts attest the importance of the chronology of the Untersiebenbrunn-Coşovenii de Jos cultural horizon for the dating of the Pietroasa treasure. The problem of this chronology can be solved in many ways. Identical or almost identical parallels with the fibulae decorated in polychrome style from Untersiebenbrunn (Fig. 13:1-2) exist in the Simleul Silvaniei hoard (Fig. 2:1) and in the finds from Kerch (Hospital Street) which are dated by coins to the end of the 4th century and the beginning of the following century.[198] The typological parallels of the piece decorated with horse heads discovered at Ehrenburg[199] lead to the same conclusion, this decorative motif being typical of these objects.[200] The analysis of the typological relation of the find from Ehrenburg shows that all the related finds are dated by coins to about A.D. 400.[201]

On the other hand, this dating is confirmed by the Scandinavian variant of the culture, the Sösdala style.[202] According to research into the typological development of this style the silver fibula with rectangular plate discovered in the grave at Nyrup (Denmark)[203] represents the precursory phase of the Sösdala style.[204] The grave from Nyrup contained, among other items, a coin of Constans (337-350) reused as a pendant, and on the basis of this find, the tomb is dated to the second half of the 4th century. In consequence of this the Sösda style, belonging to a typological phase which is later than the fibula from the grave found at Nyrup, should be dated to the end of the 4th century and the beginning of the following century.

Consequently all the finds known by us at present argue in favour of the dating of the Untersiebenbrunn horizon to the end of the 4th century and the beginning of the following century. The objects and the stylistic links between the Pietroasa treasure and the Untersiebenbrunn-Coşovenii de Jos culture support the hypothesis that the Pietroasa treasure belongs to the first half of the 5th century.

The dating and the cultural attribution of the Pietroasa treasure is particularly conditioned by the links which can be established between the pieces of the treasure which are decorated in polychrome style and other similar pieces discovered in the cultural-geographical area characterized by the polychrome style.

We will not consider further the cabochon technique; we have referred several times to finds of pieces worked in this technique at Simleul Silvaniei (Fig. 2:1), Untersiebenbrunn (Fig. 13:1-2), Kerch (Hospital Street) etc.[205] Cabochon seems to be typical especially of the beginning of the development of the polychrome style, and continues to be in use during the entire period of its development.

On the other hand, the direct cloisonné which occupied all the surface of the object is especially typical to the first half of the 5th century.[206]

Interesting conclusions can be drawn from the study of the pierced cloisonné which occurs on the collar with hinge, fibulae and multiangular cups.

The pierced cloisonné on the small fibula and on the middle size fibulae is stylistically connected with several finds from Central and Western Europe. For example, the belt-plate found in the grave at Komárom (Hungary) (Fig. 5:5) [207] is dated by analogy with that discovered in the grave at Blučina or with others of the same type in the second half of the 5th century. [208] The same technique characterized the plate of the buckle from Bački Monostor (Yugoslavia) [209] which is associated with a type of fibula assigned to the Ostrogoths and which, according to J. Werner, is dated to about 450. [210] The buckle worked in the same technique discovered at Nestin-Srem and dating from the same period is also attributed to the Ostrogoths of Yugoslavia. [211]

As regards the problem under discussion a very close analogy can be drawn with the pendant from the princely tomb found at Wolfsheim (Fig. 16:1-8); on the back of the piece there is an inscription with the name of the Persian king Artaschatar (Ardashir). The tomb, with a strong Eastern character, is dated to the beginning of the 5th century. [212]

This decorative technique appears also on some sword-sheaths dating from the second half of the 5th century, such as that found in the princely tomb from Flonheim (Fig. 6:3). [213]

The pierced translucent cloisonné which is typical of the cups or of the neck of the large fibula can be dated on the basis of two finds which provide very precise dating evidence. The princely tomb from Széged-Nagyszékés contained a cup decorated in the same technique (Fig. 5:1). All the grave-goods of the tomb are dated from the first half of the 5th century. [214] The very well known cup of Khusro II Aparwez (Fig. 16:9, A.D. 590-628) [215] which is worked in cloisonné technique, indicates, like the pendant from Wolfsheim, the Iranian origin of this technique and is an argument for the later dating of the Pietroasa treasure.

The other variant of the pierced cloisonné, observed on the collar with hinge, appears on several pieces which are typical of the Hunnic Period. A very close stylistic parallel can be drawn between the cloisonné work of the collar with hinge and that of the plate from the princely tomb at Kudinetov (Fig. 17:3), district of Terek [216] which belongs to the first half of the 5th century. [217] The same technique, but more accurately worked, is encountered on the hilt of the sword (Scramsax) discovered in the princely tomb of Pouan (Fig. 6:2) [218] dating, on the basis of the grave-goods, to the first half of the 5th century, possibly about 450. [219]

Besides other pieces, especially sword-sheaths from the Southern USSR, (Fig. 19:7-8), the closest analogy with the collar from Pietroasa is represented by the sheath-hilt of the sword from Altlussheim. [220] The cloisonné work and the decorative motif of small hearts on the piece from Altlussheim is identical with that of the collar with hinge (Fig. 18:6). [221]

The sword from Altlussheim and that from Pouan are closely connected with the swords found in Southern Russia, and for this reason F. Garscha [222] and K. Böhner later [223] considered that their origin must be located in this part of Europe. [224]

According to J. Werner, the sword from Altlussheim, as well as the pendant from Wolfsheim were produced between 420 and 450;[225] this is more dating evidence for the chronology of the Pietroasa treasure.

The decorative technique on the handles of the multiangular cups has good parallels both with the bracelet and the gold Bulla from the Desana hoard, which is attributed to the Ostrogoths of Italy and dates to the end of the 5th century and the beginning of the next century.[226]

On the other hand the different shapes of the garnets set on the pieces from the Pietroasa treasure are encountered on several finds belonging to the polychrome style. The heart-shaped garnets occur, in addition to the examples which I have mentioned, on a sword discovered in a catacomb grave at Kerch (Hospital Street),[227] and on the cup with pedestal and the patera found at Gourdon which are dated to about 450.[228] Palmettes occur on one of the swords discovered at Kerch and on the patera from Gourdon.[229] The acanthus-leaf motif which decorates the collar and the multiangular cups is also encountered on a buckle dating from between 450 and 520[230] and belonging to the Castellani (Rome) collection and on the ornamental plate of the buckle from grave 31 at Weimar; on the basis of the grave-goods (glass beaker, double-sided comb and bronze cauldron), this grave belongs to group II of the chronology established by B. Schmidt, that is to say in absolute chronology to 450-520.[231]

All these parallels are arguments in support of my hypothesis concerning the chronology and the cultural attribution of the Pietroasa treasure within the polychrome style. That the Pietroasa treasure dates from the first half of the 5th century is also confirmed by the presence of garnets in the shape of sticks with concave flutings on one of the multiangular cups. This technical feature is of a great importance for the problem under discussion. Sticks, but with straight flutings, are encountered besides the examples we have mentioned (Apahida I and II), also on swords from the Southern USSR which are dated to the first half of the 5th century and on the sword from Pouan.[232]

The buckle decorated with sticks of the same type and dated to the 5th-6th centuries A.D., which has been found in the Frankish cemetery at Tressan represents another argument for the dating of the Pietroasa treasure in the 5th century.

Finally, to conclude the discussion on the polychrome style of the Pietroasa treasure we will deal with decorative detail which appears on the neck of the large fibula. In addition to the decoration with pierced cloisonné work, the neck of the fibula is decorated with small round recesses filled with precious stones. The same decorative system is encountered on the plate found in the grave with artificially deformed skull at Gyöngyösapáti (Hungary) dating from the first half of the 5th century (Fig. 4:32).[234]

CHAPTER 5

THE HISTORICAL BACKGROUND

The historical interpretation of the results of the archaeological analysis of the contents of the Pietroasa treasure can provide new evidence for the solution of the complex problem concerning this impressive artistic monument from North-East Wallachia. The history of the North-Danubian regions from the 4th-5th centuries A.D. may be divided into two phases. The first phase is characterized by the events which took place before the appearance of the Huns, and the second one comprises the period of the Hunnic supremacy over the Carpathian basin; from the archaeological point of view these phases covered the periods before and after the appearance of the polychrome style in the North-Danubian areas.

a) <u>The historical background before the penetration of the culture characterized by the polychrome style</u>

The treaty concluded between the Goths and Constantine in 332 meant in fact the first official legislation of the relations between the Empire and the Barbarians to the North of the Danube.[235] According to this treaty the Goths, together with the Taifali, were employed as <u>foederati</u> on tasks on the Danubian frontier defences and were obliged to provide military forces for the wars waged by the Romans, receiving subsidies, <u>annonae foederaticae,</u> consisting of food and money in return for their service.[236] According to the coin-finds, it seems that the <u>annonae foederaticae</u> were usually paid in kind. The distribution map of the coin-finds (Fig. 8) in Moldavia and especially in Wallachia from the 4th century shows a surprising scarcity of coins of gold and silver; the number of bronze coin finds also do not reveal a particular affluence in money due to this treaty. This situation is attested until the end of the 4th century; coins of silver disappear, while the number of the gold coins increases substantially in the period Valentinian II-Theodosius II, after a short period of interruption of currency-circulation (378-383) owing to the troubles caused by the penetration of the Huns into these regions.[237]

The treaty concluded in 332 was guaranteed with hostages from the Gothic aristocracy sent to Constantinople. According to I. Schmidt,[238] Athanaric's father was among them. These peaceful relations lasted for 35 years. Sometimes the Goths forgot the clauses of the treaty; the sources mention conflicts on the Danube, such as that in the time of the emperor Julian, but these conflicts are of little importance and Julian says: "The traders in slaves from Galatia suffice for the Goths, who are sold by them, regardless of their social rank" (Ammianus Marcellinus, XXII, 7, 8-9).

The central event of Eastern imperial policy in this period is without doubt the war against the Persians in 339-361 continuing into the time of the emperor

Julian and ending in 363 in the time of Jovian. Valentinian was proclaimed emperor at Nicaea on 26 February after the death of Jovian at Dadastana on 17 February 364. His brother Valens was proclaimed Augustus at Constantinople on 28 March. A very significant event for the history of the Empire took place at Nis, a few months later, for the two emperors divided the army and the Empire between them, Valentinian taking the Western part together with Illyria and Valens the Eastern area including Thrace. One of the purposes of this division was to establish an equilibrium between the Western army which was much stronger than the Eastern one, which was considered to be inferior to the other during the whole of the 4th century.[239] This relatively precarious situation of the Eastern army was due to the fact that the Eastern regions of the Empire were not under strong pressure caused by excessive dangers during the 4th century. Owing to these administrative and military reforms the Empire of Valens obtained a considerable number of German and Gaulish soldiers who were famous for their military capacity, but the Eastern army was not obliged in its turn to send soldiers to the West.[240] This situation of the Eastern army lasted until 369-371.

The Goths began to organize campaigns on a large scale in the time of Valens.[241] The Goths helped the pretender Procopius against Valens and after the defeat and execution of Procopius (May 366) they attempted to justify their attitude by invoking the treaty concluded with Constantine. Valens refuted this justification and decided to organize a punitive expedition (Ammianus Marcellinus, XXVII, 5, 1; Eunapius fr. 37; Zosimus, IV, 10) which finally became a real war lasting with interruptions for three years (367-369) and came to an end with the famous treaty concluded at Noviodunum. The treaty was signed by Valens, for the Romans and by Athanaric "iudex potentissimus" (Themistius, X, 133-140; Ammianus Marcellinus, XXVII, 5, 6) for the Goths. This treaty in fact meant the annulment of the treaty concluded in Constantine's time. According to Themistius, the frontier between the Goths and Romans was established on the Danube, the subsidies ceased and commercial exchange was confined to two markets. Consequently the Goths, and the territory inhabited by them, was considered as being outside the Empire in contrast to the period of Constantine, when the territories situated to the North of the Danube were component parts of the Empire (as is suggested by Julian, Caesares, 24).

One of the most important phenomena for the history of the North-Danubian area from this period was certainly the diffusion of Christianity both into the Gothic[242] and indigenous world.[243] We will not discuss the details of this problem but the information referring to the spread of Christianity contains interesting data with regard to the different groups existing within Gothic society. The most important details concerning this problem result from study of the events connected with the two persecutions of the Christians by Athanaric. According to Socrates (IV, 33, 7) the first persecution (348-349) was provoked by the fact that "Wulfila preached Christianity not only among the Barbarians under the rule of Fritigern, but also among those under the rule of Athanaric". But the main reason for the persecution was not "the humiliation of the ancestral belief" (Socrates, IV, 33, 7). Both persecutions, from 348-349 and 369-372 represented, basically, anti-Roman measures. By these persecutions, the conservative faction led by Athanaric[244] tried to stop the spread of Roman influences among the Gothic and native population and to oppose the ideological current which was extremely dangerous to the very existence of the tribal system typical of Gothic society of that time.[245]

On the other hand the same sources mention the existence of another faction, "democratic" in the view of Várady,[246] led by Fritigern. The extremist group of this faction, which embraced the Arian form of Christianity, crossed into the Empire immediately after 348; the majority of Fritigern's faction crossed into the Empire probably in 368, before the third campaign of Valens.[247]

Was the authority of Athanaric (expressed by "iudex potentissimus") exerted effectively over all the Visigoths? The events outlined seem rather to indicate a weakening of Athanaric's authority; the situation of the Goths became more and more precarious after the conclusion of the peace treaty of Noviodunum.

With regard to the problem of locating the areas under the control of the two leaders, the information concerning the campaigns of Valens from 368 and 369 contains some suggestive data. The campaign which took place, probably in Wallachia, in 367, would indicate that Athanaric exercised his authority over this territory.[248] The fact that the treaty of 369 was concluded at Noviodunum allow us to locate the centre of the power of Athanaric in the North-East of Wallachia and the South-East of Moldavia. The information connected with the second persecution of the Christians by Athanaric when the priest Sava was drowned in the river Musaios, very probably the Buzău, (Acta Sanctorum, Avril, II, 7) leads to the same conclusion.

In these conditions it seems that Fritigern, recognizing the authority of Athanaric as iudex potentissimus, exercised control over the Southern area of Wallachia. The fact that Fritigern asked Valens for military help before the conclusion of the peace treaty,[249] demonstrates the weakening of the authority of Athanaric within the Gothic world. Even the conclusion of the treaty was connected with the pressure exerted by Fritigern,[250] in spite of the fact that Athanaric signed the peace treaty in the name of all the Visigoths. Valens, believing that equilibrium was restored on the Danube, after the victory against the Goths, sent a large contingent of troops to Valentinian I. This reshuffle of forces from 369-371 [251] brought about disastrous consequences at the battle of Adrianople (378).

b) The historical background of the development stage of the polychrome style

The years after the end of the war between Valens and the Goths are characterized by the consequences of the appearance of the Huns in the areas situated to the East of Romania. Owing to the pressure exerted by the Huns a part of the Ostrogoths, the group led by Withimir, after his death ruled by Alatheus and Saphrax, and the whole of the Visigoths were forced to retreat to the Danube. Athanaric withdrew between the Prut and the Siret, after attempting a last resistance on the Dniester; and he built there a huge defensive vallum. On the basis of the interpretation of the sources, Várady[252] suggests that the majority of the Visigoths departed from Athanaric in that moment. The crossing of the Danube, which took place in the summer of 376, brought about important consequences for the Empire. Remaining consistent in his anti-Roman principles, Athanaric withdrew to Caucaland (Ammianus Marcellinus XXXI, 4, 13) after the Ostrogothic group lead by Alatheus and Saphrax and the Visigothic group under the rule of Farnobius had not been allowed to pass into the Empire (Ammianus Marcellinus, XXXI, 4, 13). They eventually crossed the Danube during the riot of the Visigoths in 377.

Some researchers identified the region to which Athanaric had to retreat with the Banat,[253] but more probably it should be located in the region of Buzau.[254] At present, there is no archaeological evidence to attest the presence of the Goths in the Banat area.

The crossing of the Visigoths and of groups of Ostrogoths into the Empire represents an event without precedent in the history of the Empire. For the first time a large number of Germans were settled as foederati inside the Empire. The settling of the Visigoths in the Empire, more precisely in Thrace, posed extraordinary problems of organization for the Roman authorities. The incapacity of the authorities together with the abuses of the Comites per Thracias, Lupicinus and Maximus, eventually provoked the second Gothic war (377-382) which ended during the rule of Theodosius I in 382. An event of great importance for the Pietroasa treasure preceded the conclusion of the peace treaty. The old iudex potentissimus Athanaric together with his suite crossed into the Empire in the winter of 380/381. The principal reason which determined the anti-Roman Athanaric to take this decision was the conspiracy organized among the Goths remaining with him.[255] In consequence of this conspiracy he was forced to leave the North-Danubian regions, and we know that he was accompanied by a small number of people. All these facts attest once again the considerable diminution of Athanaric's sphere of domination. In these conditions, the idea that Athanaric buried this treasure (which would belong to the whole Gothic people) seems to be without historical evidence.

Athanaric received full honours, even the emperor coming to greet him. This attitude of Theodosius can be understood in the light of the war against the Goths which was in full spate at that time. By the honours paid to the pagan Athanaric, the Christian Roman emperor had in view two aims. Firstly, he wanted to impress and to attract the Visigoths to a diplomatic solution of the conflict. On the other hand, in the view of Theodosius I, the anti-Arianism of Athanaric could be used as a means of attracting the Arian Goths to Orthodox beliefs.[257]

The treaty was concluded at Constantinople, on 3 October 382, after the oldest general of Theodosius, Saturninus "magister militum" had carried on long diplomatic negotiations. The Goths received the status of foederati and were settled in Thrace; they kept their own leaders and constitution.

As a consequence of these events the majority of the Visigoths crossed to the South of the Danube. The native population, preserving its traditional way of life, remained to the North of the Danube, where a new population, the Ostrogoths led by Odotheus and probably under Hunnic domination, made their appearance at the same time. This is the time when a new population makes its appearance in the Eastern regions of Romania;[257] they are the bearers of a new culture which is characterized by, among other things, the polychrome style, which I believe is connected with the Pietroasa treasure

Considering the importance of this moment, we will deal a little more with it. Zosimus (IV, 35) showed that the army of Odotheus consisted not only of the population living beyond the Ister but also of some of the most unknown and farthest peoples; after this somewhat general information he is more precise, which is of great importance for the history of the native population to the North of the Danube. So far as I know this information has not previously been used to the extent of its real importance. Zosimus says: "A Scythian people appeared beyond the Ister about that time; they were unknown to all the shepherds from there; the local barbarians call them Greutungs....." (IV, 38).

Since the large majority of the Visigoths were established to the South of the Danube in that time, the natives, whose principal occupation was pastoral farming, must be identified with the indigenous population. This information is connected with the reference to the Carpodacian attack of 381 (Zosimus, IV 34): "Theodosius repelled the Sciri and the Carpodacians mixed with Huns and defeated them, and forced them to cross the Ister and to go back to their places". It allows us to suggest that the local shepherds should be identified with the Carpodacians who are well attested archaeologically. With regards to the Sciri and the Huns mentioned by Zosimus, they were probably the first elements of a new ethnic wave of migratory peoples advancing from the East to the Danubian regions and belonging, like the Ostrogoths (the Greutungs) to the large ethnic conglomeration represented by the Hunnic confederacy.

A process of permanent infiltration of new peoples coming from the East began at this time. In 390, the Visigoths who had retired to Macedonia after the defeat of Maximus in 388, made contact with the barbarians mentioned by Claudian on the Danube, who penetrated into Macedonia in 391. In the view of Várady, which differs from that of Birt or L. Schmidt, this information is no simple poetic licence, but refers to "the advance troops of the group of Uldis".[258] At the point we merely mention the Hunnic presence on the Danubian frontier of the Empire in 391 and 392.

The Huns provoked new disturbances on the boundary of the Empire during the Visigothic riot of 395. The main source for these events is Claudian who gives a detailed description of "this first and more important manoeuvre of Uldis" and which, according to the view of Várady, was at the same time as the expedition of the Eastern Huns into Syria, when they reached Antioch.[259] This manoeuvre could be, as we have attempted to show when studying the patera, of some importance for the history of the Pietroasa treasure.

The situation on the Danubian frontier of the Empire was restored due to the military and organisational capacity of the magister peditum Stilicho.

In about 400 Gainas the Goth, whose military activity had provoked serious disturbances in the Balkan Peninsula, attempted to return to the North of the Danube, but was killed by the Huns of Uldis (Zosimus, V, 22).

The central event of these years was without doubt the great invasion of the Ostrogoths, led by Radagais. It was in fact, "the first group of Ostrogothic origin under the Hunnic suzerainty who moved to the West".[260] They were defeated by Stilicho at Fiesole in 406.

The literary and archaeological sources record a new Hunnic invasion (402/409) of the troops led by Uldis, which took place on the Lower Danube.[261] The problem of locating the centre of Hunnic power at this time is of great importance for the cultural and historical attribution of some groups of antiquities, among them the Pietroasa treasure, which have been found in Romania. On the basis of study of Olympiodorus' embassy in 413 and of other sources, Várady concluded that the centre of power should be located to the North of the mouths of the Danube.[262] The information concerning Theotimus, the "Scythian" bishop of Tomis who preached Christianity among the Huns (Sozomen, His., ecl. VII) or the sources which mention the fortress of Carsius in Thrace (=Carsium) as being under Hunnic domination,[263] lead to the same conclusion.

The numerous raids South of the Danube which took place when the centre of gravity was situated to the North of the Danube suggests that Wallachia and Oltenia[264] were under Hunnic control. In the light of this historical context, the coin-circulation which we have mentioned earlier is explicable. The increase in the number of gold coins during the first half of the 5th century should be connected with the high subsidies which the Empire was forced to pay to the Huns, especially after the treaty concluded with the western Empire in 416.[265]

The shifting of the centre of gravity towards the West took place about 420. The conclusion of the treaty between the external Huns led by Rua and the Western Empire in 425 is a consequence of the Hunnic expansion towards the West. One of the requests of the external Huns refers to the dissolution of the federates in Pannonia and Valeria. The removal of these federates, (according to Várady, they can be identified with the group of Alatheus and Saphrax) took place in about 427.[266]

The peaceful establishment of the Huns in Pannonia took place after 427. The new situation was formalised by the treaty concluded between the Huns and the Western Empire in 433. According to this treaty, the Huns settled as <u>foederati</u> in Pannonia and the title of <u>magister militum</u> was bestowed upon Attila. The treaty also stipulated among other conditions that a tribute of 700 pounds of gold must be annually paid and that the markets could be used both by the Huns and the Romans (Priscus Panites, <u>On the embassies</u>... p. 211 De Boor/1).

The tribute and the freedom to trade gained by the Huns shows that Hunnic society tended to integrate into the Roman economic system. The numerous expeditions of the Huns into the Empire can[267] probably be explained by the same reason or by their insatiable greed for objects and ornaments of gold. Priscus points out many times the richness of the leading class of the Huns. Even the bishop of Margus "searched for the places where the kings' fortune was lodged and plundered their hidden treasures "and this fact brought about the campaign of 442 (Priscus, <u>On the embassies,</u> De Boor, p. 575). This explains very clearly the exceptional richness of the Pietroasa treasure. This phenomenon is not known within Gothic society to the North of the Danube in the 4th century.

The shift in the centre of gravity to the Theiss (Tisa) plain does not mean that control over the territories on the Lower Danube ceased. We can deduce from the information given by Priscus (On the embassies ... p. 112, De Boor, 2) that these territories continued to belong to the Hunnic sphere of domination, after 433.

We should emphasise that the Huns certainly played a predominant part within the Hunnic state, but besides the Huns, other populations belonging to this ethnic conglomerate played a role of great importance in the political and military life of the Hunnic Empire. Attila attempted to secure control over his huge empire by means of these peoples and their leaders.[268] The distribution of gold objects worked in polychrome style (Fig. 8) is very eloquent in this respect. In my opinion the massive concentration of finds in the Buzau area (Cîlnau, Gheraseni, Pietroasa, Pîrscov) are arguments in support of the hypothesis that the centre of power which assumed control over the North-Danubian territory should be located in this geographical zone of Wallachia.

The death of Attila (453) and then the battle of Nedao brought about the eventual collapse of the Hunnic Empire which "accomplished an historical necessity, by creating new possibilities for some ethnic groups from the barbaricum to reach a superior stage of civilization within the sphere of Mediterranean culture".[269]

These events brought about changes of great importance in the history and culture of the Carpathian basin. The major consequences of these events can give sufficient reasons for the hypothesis that the Pietroasa treasure was buried in the middle of the 5th century.

CONCLUSION

The archaeological analysis of the component pieces of the Pietroasa treasure, combined with the information given by the literary sources, support the dating of the treasure to the first half of the 5th century.

The runic inscription and the wearing of fibulae argue in favour of a Germanic attribution,[270] probably to the Ostrogoths,[271] who were the sole Germanic population belonging to the Hunnic confederacy, and who rise to prominence at this date. The structure of the treasure confirms the information of the literary sources as to the political importance of the Ostrogoths within the State organization led by the Huns.[272] They formed an upper stratum securing control over the territories inhabited by the Daco-Roman native population.

On the other hand the patera, the oenochoe-jug, and the small and middle-size fibulae, reflect close relations and diverse connections with the Roman Empire. The decorative technique of the neck and of the pedestal of the oenochoe-jug represents one of the characteristic elements of this Late Roman industry which worked for the "Barbaricum". The catch-system of the small and middle-size fibulae borrowed from the cross-bow fibulae, dress-ornaments typical of the garments of the superior civilian and military staff of the Empire together with the type of fibula, which is in fact an imitation of a dress-ornament of the Imperial costume, suggests the existence of very complex economic and political relationships.

All the gifts and especially the honours granted to the Hunnic leading stratum, probably the Ostrogoths in the present context, suggest that the Imperial Court tended to maintain a formal authority over some of its lost territories.[273]

On the other hand the imitation of the imperial fashion and the adoption of some Roman cultural objects reflect the contact between two different social structures, but at the same time express the tendency of the barbarian world to integrate into Roman economic, cultural and political systems.[274] This economic, cultural and political dialogue also exerted a special influence on the consolidation of the North-Danubian Roman tradition.

The burial of the treasure in about 450 is an archaeological reflection of the historical events connected with the disappearance of the Hunnic state. For the North-Danubian Roman tradition a new stage of assimilation of external influences began in the first half of the 5th century, and the peak of this process takes place in the period of Justinian.

NOTES

1. R. Hachmann, Die Goten und Skandinavien, Berlin 1970, p. 150; the work of Oskar Montelius, Die älteren Kulturperioden im Orient und Europa, Vol. I, Die Methode, Stockholm 1903, in which several basic principles (especially the typology) of the archaeology are established, are published after the death of Odobescu; see below n. 2.

2. Al. Odobescu, Le trésor de Pétrossa, Historique-Description. Étude sur l'orfévrerie antique, Paris 1889-1900, vol. I (1889), vol. II (1896), vol. III (1900); and Al. Odobescu, Opere, vol. IV. Tezaurul de la Pietroasa, Bucharest, 1976 (introduction, ocommentaries and notes by Mircea Babeş. Archaeological studies by Radu Harhoiu and Gheorghe Diaconu).

3. C. Diculescu, Die Wandalen und Goten in Ungarn and Rumänien, Mannus - Bibl. No. 34, Würzburg, 1923, p. 96 and following.

4. R. Hachmann, op.cit., p. 11.

5. M. C. Soutzo, Dacia, 3-4, 1927-1932, pp. 628-631.

6. Gogo Müller-Knales in H. Reinerth, Vorgeschichte der deutschen Stämme, vol. III, Die Ostgermanen, Leipzig, 1941, p. 1201.

7. J. Werner, Beiträge zur Archäologie des Attilareiches, München, 1956, p. 80.

8. Ecaterina Dunăreanu-Vulpe, Analele rom.-sov., 10, 1956, 3, pp. 5-12; idem in vol. general editor, G. Oprescu, Studii asupra tezaurului restituit de URSS, Bucharest, 1958, p. 54; idem, Tesaurul de la Pietroasa, Bucharest, 1967, p. 16, 51.

9. We refer especially to N. Fettich, Germania, 16, 1932, pp. 300-304; idem, Der zweite Schatz von Szilágysomlyó, Arch-Hung, 8, 1932.

10. I. Nestor in Istoria României, vol. I, Bucharest, 1960, pp. 698-699.

11. R. Theodorescu, Pagini de arta veche românească de la origini pînă la sfîrsitul secolului al XVI-1ea, Bucharest, 1970, p. 21 and following.

12. O. Iliescu, RESEE, 3, 1965, 1-2, 269-281 with the bibliography.

13. Z. Szekely, FoliaArch, 5, 1944, 95-101.

14. I. Nestor, op.cit., p. 699.

15. N. Fettich, ArchHung, 8, 1932, p. 67.

16. K. Horedt, Germania, 50, 1972, 1-2, 219, note 1.

17. C. Preda, SCIVA, 26, 1975, 4, p. 444.

18. J. Hubert, J. Pocher, W. F. Volbach, L'Europe des invasions, Paris, 1967, p. 216.

19. B. Arrhenius, Granatschmuck und Gemmen aus nordischen Funden des frühen Mittelalters, Stockholm, 1971.

20. Ibid., p. 18, note 3.

21. R. Theodorescu, Un mileniu de artă la Dunărea de Jos, Bucharest, 1976, p. 59.

22. M. Rostovtzeff, Iranians and Greeks in South Russia, Oxford, 1922, p. 186.

23. Brenner, 8, BerRGK, 1912, Frankfurt, 1915, p. 271; R. Zahn, Spätantike Silbergefässe, Amtl. Bericht, 38, 1916-1917, col. 276, 278, 283-284.

24. N. Beleaev, Seminarium Kondakovianum, 3, 1929, p. 112.

25. A. Alföldi, Germania, 16, 1932, p. 136.

26. N. Fettich, Germania, 16, 1932, p. 302; idem, ArchHung, 8, 1932, p. 70.

27. C. Daicoviciu, AISC, Cluj, 3, 1936-1940, p. 250, note 1.

28. H. Arbmann, MeddelandenLund, 1947-1948, pp. 97-136.

29. Ibid., p. 135.

30. K. Böhner, Bonner Jahrb, 148, 1948, p. 230.

31. W. Holmquist, Germanic Art during the first milenium A.D., Stockholm, 1955, p. 29 and following.

32. K. Horedt, AMN, 6, 1959, 549-551.

33. K. Horedt, D. Protase, AMN, 7, 1970, 185-201; ibid., Germania, 48, 1970, 1-2, 85-98 (the hoard found at Someșeni in 1963); ibid., Germania, 50, 1972, 1-2, 174-220 (Apahida II, princely tomb discovered in 1968).

34. K. Horedt, AMN, 6, 1959, 550.

35. Idem, Germania, 50, 1972, 1-2, 217 and following.

36. N. Kondakoff, N. I. Tolstoi, S. Reinach, Antiquité de la Russie méridionale, Paris, 1891, p. 503.

37. R. Theodorescu, op.cit., p. 22.

38. E. Dunăreanu-Vulpe, in (vol. general editor, G. Oprescu) Studii asupra tezaurului restituit de URSS, Bucharest, 1958, p. 52.

39. R. Theodorescu, op.cit., p. 23.

40. V. Teodorescu, Bucharest, Materiale de istorie și muzeografie, 9, 1972, p. 91, note 47.

41. See below, appendix 1.

42. V. V. Kropotkin, Arheologia SSSR, D1-27, Moscow 1970, p. 87; p. 205, fig. 53/2.

43. F. Kuchenbuch, SaalburgJahrb, 13, 1954, p. 16; J. Tejral, Mähren im V. Jahrhundert, Prague, 1973, pp. 15-16 with the whole discussion concerning the dating of the complexes found at Kerch, Hospital Street to the end of the 4th century.

44. E. Dunăreanu-Vulpe, Tezaurul de la Pietroasa, Bucharest 1967, p. 29; R. Theodorescu, op.cit., p. 25.

45. G. Nicolăescu-Plopsor, H. Zeiss, Germania, 17, 1933, pp. 272-285, pl. 24, fig. 1 and 2.

46. With regard to the chronology of the Unterseibenbrunn-Cosovenii de Jos culture, see below,

47. M. I. Artamonov, Sokrovisca skifskih kurganov v sobranii Gosudarstevenovo Ermitaja, Leningrad-Prague, 1966, p. 110 and fig. 146.

48. E. Dunăreanu-Vulpe in vol. Studii..., p. 51; see also Al. Odobescu, Le trésor, vol. I, p. 116, fig. 43.

49. A. Banck, Byzantine Art in the collection of the USSR, Moscow, 1966, fig. 83 and 343 and following.

50. E. Vulpe, Tezaurul..., p. 30.

51. B. Mitrea, C. Preda, Necropole din sec. al IV-1ea din Muntenia, Bucharest, 1966, p. 92; which mention also that a hand-made vessel was discovered on the occasion of the ground-survey made at the find-spot of the vessel.

52. Gh. Diaconu, Tîrgsor. Necropola din sec. III-IV, Bucharest, 1965, p. 140, p. 165, pl. XXV/1, 4.

53. Ibid., p. 40.

54. G. Meszarós, ArhErt, 97, 1, 1970, p. 81, fig. 16. The grave found at Regöly is dated from the end of the 4th century and the beginning of the 5th century; ibid., p. 92. Another jug of the same type has been discovered in the cemetery at Popuzu, commune of Balaciu, district of Ialomița, in which double-sided bone combs have also been found; the combs date the archaeological context to the end of the 4th century (information Gh. Diaconu).

55. M. Rostovtzeff, op.cit., p. 138 and following; p. 186; N. Kondakoff, N. I. Tolstoi, S. Reinach, op.cit., p. 504.

56. N. Fettich, ArhErt, 45, 1931, p. 304. In the light of present research the relation between the cauldron of Gundesturp, which is Celtic (see Ole Klindt Jensen, Gundestrupkedelen, Copenhagen, 1961) and the vessels found at Simleul Silvaniei and Peitroasa cannot be supported. The sole element of connection consists of their sacred character which has been stressed also by Odobescu; see, in this sense, also G. Nagy, A Magyar Története, I, Budapest, 1895, p. CCXIV and following.

57. M. C. Soutzo, op.cit., p. 630.

58. R. Theodorescu, op.cit., p. 26; E. Dunărea-Vulpe, op.cit., p. 18 and following.

59. Ch. de Linas, Les origines de l'orfèvrerie cloisonné, Recherches sur les divers genres d'incrustation de joillerie et l'art des métaux précieux, Arras-Paris, 1877-1887.

60. M. von Heland, The golden bowl from Pietroasa, Acta Universitatis Stockholmiensis, Stockholm Studies of Art, 24, Stockholm, 1973.

61. Ibid., p. 65, 89.

62. Ibid., p. 65 and following.

63. Ibid., p. 99 and following.

64. J. Bidez, Julian der Abtrünnige, München 1940, p. 297 and following.

65. See below, p. 33.

66. With regard to the religious policy of Julian, see J. Bidez, op.cit., pp. 234-237, 260-326.

67. E. Vulpe, op.cit., p. 32.

68. Ibid., loc.cit.

69. J. Hampel, Alterthümer des frühen Mittelalter in Ungarn, Braunschweig, 1905, vol. 3, pl. 14/a,c; Al. Odobescu, Le Trésor..., vol. I, p. 218, fig. 92.

70. M. Chaucey-Ross, Catalogue of the byzantine and early mediaeval antiquities in the Dumbarton Oaks Collection, vol. II, Washington, 1965, pl. 38/47 and p. 46 and following.

71. K. Horedt, AMN, 6, 1969, p. 550.

72. J. Werner, op.cit., München, 1956, pp. 86-87 point out the presence of silver jugs in the graves from the Hunnic period at Concești or Bolshaya Kamenec.

73. S. Dumitrașcu, Tezaurul de la Tăuteni-Bihor, Oradea, 1975.

74. E. Keller, Germania, 1-2, 45, 1967, p. 116; see pp. 117-118 the list of the plain collars with loop and hook of massive gold and the distribution-map at p. 115.

75. A. Petre, Materiale, 8, 1962, p. 572, fig. 7.

76. E. Keller, op.cit., p. 116, note 39.

77. M. Nagy, ArhErt, 97, 2, 1970, p. 313.

78. The other massive gold collars of this type found in Romania, see K. Horedt, Germania, 25, 1941, p. 121, pl. 21/10. Uileacul Simleului, district Sălaj, see ArhErt, 22, 1902, p. 432, come from isolated finds. Their chronological and cultural attribution is based on the finds in closed complexes.

79. J. Werner, op.cit., pl. 59.

80. N. Fettich, ArchHung, 32, 1953; Against the interpretation of the burial ritual proposed by N. Fettich (cremation grave), but not against the dating, see I. Bona, ActaArch, 23, 1971, p. 267 and following.

81. K. Sági, ArhErt, 82, 1955, pp. 183-189.

82. W. Kubitschek, JahrbfAltertumskunde, 5, 1911, p. 41, fig. 8.

83. E. Salin, A. France-Lannord, Gallia, 14, 1, 1956, p. 74, fig. 24; the dating of the grave, p. 75.

84. For the whole problem, see M. Isbăşescu, Revista de filolologie romanica si germanica, 1, 1957, p. 119 and following.

85. R. Neumeister, Mitth. d. Central-Komiss., Vienna, 13, 1868, pp. 115-117.

86. M. Isbăşescu, op.cit., p. 126.

87. R. Loewe, Indogermanische Forschungen, 1910, pp. 203-208.

88. C. Marstrander, Nors Tidskrift vor Spragvidenskap, 3, 1929, pp. 38-67.

89. For the runic inscriptions found in Romania see also Gh. Diaconu, Dacia, N.S., XX, 1976, pp. 269-271.

90. W. F. Volbach, Elfenbeinarbeiten der Spätantike und des frühen Mittelalters, Mainz, 1952, p. 32 and following; pl. 8/35; R. Delbruck, Spätantike Kaiserporträts. Vom Konstantinus Magnus bis zum Ende des Westreichs, Berlin-Leipzig, 1933, pl. 94; Al. Odobescu, Le trésor ..., vol. I, p. 318, fig. 121.

91. E. Dunăreanu-Vulpe, op.cit., p. 88; R. Theodorescu, op.cit., p. 28.

92. M. I. Artamonov, op.cit., fig. 205: the collar from the Scythian tomb found at Kul Oba which differs in technique from the collar from Pietroasa; see also M. Babeş, in Al. Odobescu, Opere, vol. IV, Bucharest, 1976, p. 974.

93. G. Bovini, Ravenna. Ville d'art, Ravenna, 1970, p. 39, p. 45; see also K. Horedt, Germania, 50, 1-2, 1972, p. 215, note 111, similar objects but with other purposes in Al. Odobescu, Le trésor..., vol. 1, p. 454, fig. 177; p. 460, fig. 183; p. 460, fig. 184- p. 461, fig. 185; p. 461, fig. 186.

94. For the whole problem concerning the genesis of this type of fibula, see N. Fettich, Germania, 16, 1932, p. 300 and following; A. Alföldi, ArchHung, 9, 1932 p. 39 points out that the zoomorphic motif became geometrical on the small fibula; see also J. M. Santa Olalla, Germania, 20, 1936, p. 50, who proposes also an influence from the zoomorphic fibulae of the Late imperial period exerted on the genesis of the fibulae from Pietroasa which are dated to the end of the 4th century; he based his hypothesis upon an eagle-shaped fibula found in the fort at Saalburg, see Jacobi, Germania, 16, 1932, p. 161, fig. 6. It seems however that

the affiliation proposed by Fettich must be admitted. The adoption of the eagle pattern, as we will attempt to show below, came about in another way. In this sense also H. Kühn, <u>IPEK,</u> 13-14, 1939-1940, p. 138.

95. N. Fettich, <u>ArchHung,</u> 8, 1932, pl. VIII/8; pl. IX/1; see also N. Beleaev, <u>op.cit.,</u> p. 129.

96. N. Fettich, <u>Germania,</u> 16, 1932, p. 304.

97. <u>Idem, ArchHung,</u> 8, 1932, pl. XVIII, XX, XXIII etc.

98. F. Kuchenbuch, <u>op.cit.,</u> p. 16; I. P. Zasetkaia, <u>SA,</u> 2, 1968, p. 56.

99. E. Salin, A. France-Lannord, <u>Monuments et Mémoires,</u> 43, 1949, pl. XIV.

100. W. Kubitschek, <u>op.cit.,</u> pl. I/1-2.

101. F. Kuchenbuch, <u>op.cit., loc.cit.</u>

102. E. Keller, <u>Die spätrömischen Grabfunde aus Südbayern,</u> München, 1971, p. 34, pl. 5/13.

103. <u>Ibid.,</u> p. 34, pl. 5/12.

104. <u>Ibid.,</u> p. 35 (type 5); p. 52 and following (type 6) . For the chronology of type 6, see also R. Harhoiu, <u>SCIV,</u> 24, 2, 1973, p. 321 and following.

105. B. Arrhenius, <u>op.cit.,</u> p. 106 and following; J. Hubert, J. Pocher, M. V. Volbach, <u>op.cit.,</u> p. 220, fig. 233.

106. Al. Tzigara-Sarmucaş, <u>op.cit.,</u> p. 772 identified this zoomorphic pattern as a parrot.

107. J. Werner, <u>op.cit.,</u> p. 73; and following; for the presence of this pattern on the pottery see G. Meszáros, <u>op.cit.,</u> p. 81, fig. 16.

108. B. Piotrovsky, <u>Or des Scythes,</u> Paris, 1975, pp. 136-22.

109. <u>Ibid.,</u> p. 138/29.

110. H. Kühn, <u>op.cit.,</u> p. 138.

111. M. I. Artamonov, <u>op.cit.,</u> p. 105, fig. 74.

112. <u>Ibid.,</u> fig. 91-92.

113. B. Piotrokovsky, <u>op.cit.,</u> p. 179/131.

114. <u>Ibid.,</u> p. 179/132.

115. <u>Ibid.,</u> p. 184/150.

116. H. Kühn, <u>op.cit.,</u> p. 139; J. Werner, <u>op.cit.,</u> p. 70.

117. <u>Ibid.,</u> p. 69 and following and p. 79 note 4, mention other examples in this sense.

118. A. Alföldi, <u>Germania,</u> 16, 1932, p. 136.

119. J. Werner, <u>op.cit.,</u> p. 73.

120. Ibid., p. 80.

121. N. Fettich, op.cit., p. 304; J. M. Santa Olalla, op.cit., p. 50.

122. D. Brown, Antiquity, 46, 1972, p. 113 and following.

123. Ibid., p. 113, fig. 1; p. 114, fig. 2.

124. Ibid., p. 115, fig. 3.

125. See supra, note 123 and note 124.

126. Ibid., p. 115; N. Beleaev, op.cit., p. 107; the twisted chains for the pendants cannot be more precisely dated. This type of chain is encountered in the Scythian milieu, see M. I. Artamonov, op.cit., fig. 214-215, fig. 221-223, fig. 326-327, and continues to appear also in the 5th century as is attested by the pectoral-chain found at Cluj-Someşeni, see D. Protase, J. Horedt, Germania, 1-2, 48, 1970, pl. 22/1-2; a general view concerning the twisted chains in H. Potratz, IPEK, 17, 1943-1948, pp. 77-103.

127. See supra, note 42.

128. R. Delbrueck, op.cit., pl. 56; N. Beleaev, op.cit., p. 110; A. Bank, op.cit., figs. 8-9.

129. N. Beleaev, op.cit., loc.cit.

130. Ibid., p. 76, fig. 15.

131. Ibid., p. 77, fig. 16; W. F. Volbach, op.cit., p. 10; pl. 10/38.

132. R. Delbrueck, op.cit., pl. 93; N. Fettich, op.cit., ArchHung, 8, 1932, p. 60, fig. 5/a,b.

133. Ibid., p. 60 and p. 60, note 1.

134. R. Delbrueck, op.cit., pp. 198-199.

135. N. Beleaev, op.cit., p. 110 and following; the fibula worn by Theodosius I on the shoulder, represented on the Missorium of this emperor dating to 388 (Madrid, Real Academia de la Historia) is suggestive in this respect, see R. Delbrueck, op.cit., pl. 94-97; see also Al. Odobescu, Le trésor..., vol. I, p. 153, fig. 72; for example a fibula of this kind occurs on a seal of the time of Maurice (582-602), see A. Bank, op.cit., fig. 118.

136. W. F. Volbach, op.cit., pl. 8/35 and p. 32; see also Al. Odobescu, Le trésor..., vol. I, p. 318, fig. 121.

137. In this respect also D. Brown, op.cit., p. 115, but he dates the treasure to the time of Athanaric.

138. Ch. de Linas, op.cit.; A. Riegl, Die spätrömische Kunstindustrie nach ihren Funden in Österreich-Ungarn, Vienna, 1901; J. Hubert, J. Pocher, W. F. Volbach, op.cit., p. 209 and following; B. Arrhenius, Reallexikon der Germanischen Altertumskunde, I, pp. 174-181.

139. We will use for the study of the polychrome style some of the results of the analysis made by B. Arrhenius, Granatschmuck..., p. 6 and following.

140. Identification M. Cîrciumaru.

141. B. Arrhenius, op.cit., p. 45.

142. Ibid., p. 27, fig. 60 b.

143. J. Werner, op.cit., pp. 61-80; M. A. Tihanova, SA, 3, 1970, p. 124 and following.

144. K. Horedt, Germania, 50, 1-2, 1972, p. 215 and note 111.

145. E. Busuioc, Dacia, N.S., 17, 1973, p. 341.

146. Largely J. Werner, Bayer Vb 1, 25, 1960, p. 172 and following, but especially p. 175, note 36 (list of buckles of this type).

147. See supra, p. 15.

148. K. Horedt, SCIV, 18, 4, 1967, p. 591.

149. J. Werner, SlovArch, 7, 1959, p. 423; the dating is based upon the analysis of the fibulae of this type found at Kosino, Gava, Tiszalök, Gyulavari, Kiskunfelekyhaza.

150. C. Bloşiu, Cercetări istorice, 5, 1974, pl. I/1-12, 14-15 (all pieces are illustrated).

151. Ibid., p. 77.

152. J. Hampel, op.cit., vol. II, pp. 42-43; vol. III, pl. 36.

153. K. Horedt, Germania, 48, 1-2, 1970, pl. 23/1-7 (sleeve-shaped pendants).

154. J. Hampel, op.cit., loc.cit.

155. K. Horedt, Germania, 1-2, 50, 1972, pl. 16-19 (decorative plates).

156. Idem, Germania, 1-2, 48, 1970, loc.cit., pl. 23/19 (rhomboid pendants).

157. Ibid., pl. 21/a, (the pectoral).

158. J. Hampel, op.cit., vol. II, p. 43.

159. K. Horedt, Germania, 50, 1-2, 1972, pl. 34/2 a-b (decorative plates belonging to the sheath of a sword - Spatha); pl. 39/3 c (a large buckle); pl. 49-50 (the appliqué has the foot in the shape of an eagle).

160. Ibid., pl. 34.

161. Idem, Untersuchungen zur Frühgeschichte Siebenbürgens, Bucharest, 1958, p. 82.

162. Idem, Germania, 1-2, 48, 1970, p. 96.

163. Idem, Germania, 50, 1-2, 1972, p. 209 and following.

164. Ibid., p. 213 table 1; the wavy cloisonné occurs both on the grave-goods from the princely tomb found at Pécs-Uszög (J. Hampel, op.cit., vol. 2, p. 372, fig. 4) and on some of the pieces discovered at Kerch, (N. Fettich, ArchHung, 32, 1953, pl. 21/4), these pieces are dated to the first half of the 5th century, see I. Bona, op.cit., p. 267 and following. On the other hand this technique is not encountered on several finds dating from the first half of the 5th century, as in the case of the princely tomb from Szeged-Nagyszéksós, see N. Fettich, op.cit., pl. I-XVII, and this situation is explicable by the differences in workshops and not in dating.

165. J. Werner, KölnerJahrb, 3, 1958, p. 57 and following., with the list of the finds of this type to which tomb 2 at Apahida must now be added. The dating of grave 2 at Apahida in the first half of the 5th century is especially based upon the presence of some nomadic elements (the appliqués in the shape of an eagle, pieces of harness) which might represent also persistence from the previous period.

166. Some graves also containing swords have recently been found at Pietroasa. These graves, dated by the coins of Constantius II are unique within the Sîntana de Mureş-Cerneahov culture. Their dating and cultural attribution must be determined by future research.

167. I. Kovacs, DolgCluj, 3, 1912, pp. 250-367; M. A. Tihanova, ArhPam, 1, 1949; B. Mitrea, C. Preda, op.cit., pp. 111-164; Gh. Diaconu, op.cit., pp. 112-133; K. Horedt, SCIV, 18, 4, 1967, pp. 575-592; I. Nestor, Dacia, N.S., 19, 1975, 9-11.

168. Em. Zaharia, N. Zaharia, Dacia, N.S., 19, 1975, pp. 201-226.

169. Ibid., p. 217, fig. 11/6.

170. W. Kutitschek, op.cit., pl. 5/11.

171. Information Gh. Diaconu.

172. V. Teodorescu et al., paper presented at the Xth session of archaeological reports, Bucharest, 1976.

173. D. Gh. Teodoru, V. Căpitanu, I. Mitrea, Carpica, 1, 1968, pp. 233-247.

174. Gh. Rădulescu, M. Ionescu, SCIV, 14, 1, 1963, p. 179, fig. 4.

175. Gh. Diaconu, op.cit., pl. 66/3; pl. 84/4; pl. 111/7 (pendants) I. Ioniţă, ArhMoldovei, 4, 1966, p. 214, fig. 19/4 (combs); for the grave at Lebeny, see R. Pusztai, Arrabona, 8, 1961, p. 112, fig. 8, for the type of comb decorated with horse heads, see S. Thomas, Arbeits- und Forschungsberichte zur sächsischen Bodendenkmalspflege, 8, 1960, p. 54 and following; R. Koch, Germania, 1, 43, 1965, p. 109 and following; Peter Petru-Thilo Ulbert, Vranje bei Sevnica. Frühchristliche Kirchenanlage auf dem Ajdovski Gradec, Ljubliana, 1975, with regard to the imitation in clay of the oenochoe-jug from Pietroasa, see supra, p. 9.

176. L. M. Rutkivska, Arheologija, Kiev, 22, 1969, pp. 149-160.

177. E. V. Vejmarn, ArhPam, 13, 1963, pp. 15-42.

178. A. K. Ambroz, Anticnye drevnosti Porodija, Moscow, 1969, pp. 262-263; J. Tejral, op.cit., p. 59; and see N. Fettich, ArchHung, 32, 1953, p. 184.

179. For this phenomenon, G. Kossack, Prunkgräber, Studien zur vor- und frühgeschichtlichen Archäologie. Festschrift für Joachim Werner. Münchner Beiträge zur Vor- und Frühgeschichte, Ergbd. 1 (1974), 3-33.

180. G. Meszarós, op.cit., loc.cit.

181. R. Ptusztai, op.cit., p. 112, fig. 8, p. 114.

182. K. Horedt, op.cit., p. 587. The author supports his theory that the Sîntana de Mureş-Cerneahov culture dates later in Transylvania, from the beginning of the 5th century by the dating of the fibulae with semi-disc variant I - at the end of the 4th century and the beginning of the 5th century. According to E. Keller, BayerVbl, 36, 1, 1971, p. 171 and p. 174, fig. 4/1-3, fibulae with semi-disc variant I - are dated in typological phase I dating only from the end of the 4th century; in the same respect, Gh. Diaconu, Dacia, N.S., 17, 1973, pp. 264-265; somewhat for the dating proposed by K. Horedt, but with other interpretations of the ethnic I. Nestor, Dacia, N.S., 19, 1975, p. 11. In the view of I. Nestor, op.cit., p. 10 and following, the group of graves in the North-West of Transylvania (Palatca, Tîrgu Mureş, Sîntana de Mureş) would belong to the early Gepidae and only the finds situated in the South-East of Transylvania (for example, Cernat) can be assigned to the Sîntana de Mureş-Cerneahov culture. At the same time the presence of the native population is attested by the cremation cemetery at Bratei, see L. Bîrzu, Continuitatea populatiei autohtone în Transilvania în secolele IV-V (Cimitirul 1 de la Bratei), Bucharest, 1973, dating from the end of the 4th century and the beginning of the following.

183. In this respect, M. Párducz, ActaArch, 26, 1974, pp. 198-199 who refutes the hypothesis put forward by I. Bona, ActaArch, 23, 1971, p. 174, that the finds at Artand were closely related to the Sîntana de Mureş-Cerneahov culture.

184. G. Tejral, op.cit., p. 46.

185. E. Keller, op.cit., p. 171 and following.

186. With regard to the problem of the whole culture, see C. Nicolăescu-Plopşor, H. Zeiss, op.cit., pp. 272-285; J. E. Forrsanders, Meddelanden, 1937, p. 11 and following; H. Geisslinger, Offa, 17-18, 1959-1961, p. 175 and following, R. Koch, Germania, op.cit., p. 109 and following and especially p. 120 with the list of the pendants of the same tupe; Ulla Lund-Hansen, Aarbger, 1969, pp. 63-102; J. Tejral, op.cit., pp. 6-18.

187. Nicolăescu-Plopsor, H. Zeiss, op.cit., pl. 24.

188. W. Kubitschek, op.cit., pl. 4/2, 4.

189. M. A. Tihanova, SA, 1, 1960, 196-204.

190. N. Aberg, Fornvännen, 1936, pp. 264-277; pl. 2/9-10, 14-19 (pieces decorated with cabochon); pl. 2/11, 13 (cloisonné buckles); pl. 3/21-23, 26; pl. 4/27-28 (pieces with engraved decoration).

191. B. Arrhenius, op.cit., p. 31; p. 40, fig. 31/a-b.

192. W. Kubitschek, op.cit., pl. I/1-7 (pieces worked in polychrome style) pl. III/1-10; pl. IV/1-10 (pieces with engraved decoration).

193. See supra, p. 10.

194. J. Hampel, op.cit., vol. 3, pl. 14/p2, o, h, w, ay.

195. With regard to the elements connecting the two hoards, see N. Fettich, ArchHung, 8, 1932, p. 66 and following. The pendants of the Untersiebenbrunn-Coşovenii de Jos type are absent from hoard 2 at Simleul Silvaniei, while the fibulae with semi-disc and elongated foot having perfect analogies in the grave from Untersiebenbrunn are present in the same hoard; for this reason, in all probability, the two treasures represent in fact a single one.

196. For this problem, see also K. Böhner, op.cit., p. 230.

197. I. P. Zasetskaia, Zolotiie ukralenia gunskoi epohi, Leningrad, 1975, p. 23, fig. 6; the very close connection between the pieces decorated in polychrome style and those with engraved decoration is confirmed by the use of the polychrome decoration on the pieces which are usually decorated by engraving. In addition to the harness-ring (above mentioned) from Kerch, we mention another similar found also at Kerch (fig. 1/10), see N. Fettich, ArchHung, 32, 1953, p. 133 and pl. 30/33-34.

198. See supra, p. 15; a shield-umbo with facets has also been discovered at Kerch, Hospital Street; it is typical of the 4th century and the beginning of the 5th century, as is suggested by analogy with the shield-umbo of Stilicho occurring on the consular dyptich from Milan, see W. F. Volbach, op.cit., pl. 19/63. This type of umbo (one piece of this type has been discovered in the district of Bistrița-Năsăud, information Gh. Marinescu) is an important piece in the cultural group Dobrodzien, which is typical of the end of the 4th century and the beginning of the 5th century. For the chronology of this cultural group, see K. Godlewski, The chronology of the later Roman and early migration periods in Central Europe, Krakow, 1970, p. 110 and pl. IV/13. The presence, apparently inexplicable, might be connected with the cultural and chronological horizon represented by the graves from the 5th century discovered at Fîntînele, district of Bistrița-Năsăud. The publication of these archaeological researches will confirm or refute this hypothesis.

199. R. Koch, op.cit., p. 109 and following.

200. Ibid., p. 111, fig. 3; the distribution of the pieces decorated with this zoomorphic motif, which appears also on one of the monuments typical of the Untersiebenbrunn-Coşovenii de Jos; the Kacin treasure, see V. P. Petrov, A. P. Kalisciuk, Materiali i Dosidjenia z arheologii Prikarpatia i Volini, 5, 1964, pp. 88-95; see also J. Tejral, op.cit., p. 17, who dates the Kacin hoard to the beginning of the 5th century.

201. R. Koch, op.cit., p. 115.

202. J. E. Forrsander, op.cit.; U. Lund-Hansen, op.cit.

203. Aarbger, 1877, p. 372; H. Norling-Christensen, Aarbger, 1956, pp. 60-61; fig. 26-27/14; U. Lund-Hansen, Inventaria Archaeologica, Denmark, Bonn 1971, sect. 8, DK 42 4 (I)/3.

204. H. Geisslinger, op.cit., p. 178 and following produces also other arguments in support of the above-mentioned dating.

205. See supra, p. 15.

206. K. Böhner, op.cit., p. 228 and following.

207. J. Hampel, op.cit., vol. 2, pp. 46-47; vol. 3, pl. 40.

208. K. Tihelka, PamArch, 54, 2, 1963, p. 471; 473, fig. 5/2; for the spur of the same type as those found at Komárom, see P. T. Kessler, W. Schellenkamp, MainzerZ, 28, 1933, p. 123 and following, with the dating in the second half of the 5th century.

209. I. Kovacevic, L'archéologie et l'histoire de la colonisation barbare des territoires des slaves du sud du IVe au VIIe s., Novi Sad, p. 67, fig. 92.

210. J. Werner, SlovArch, 7, 1959, pp. 422-439; a similar type of fibula has been discovered in Romania, in the cemetery at Botoşani-Dealu Cărămidăriei, v. Em. Zaharia, N. Zaharia, op.cit., p. 217, fig. 11/2.

211. I. Kovacevic, op.cit., p. 66, fig. 67.

212. MainzerZ, 17/19, 1922/24, p. 73 and following with older bibliography G. Behrens, Die Binger Lanschaft in der Vor-und Frühgeschichte, Mainz, 1954, p. 46, fig. 67; p. 43.

213. P. T. Kessler, V. Schnellkamp, op.cit., p. 119, fig. 2/2; N. Fettich, op.cit., pl. 32/1; pl. 33/6; B. Arrhenius, op.cit., p. 80.

214. N. Fettich, op.cit., pl. 15; pl. 17; for dating, ibid., pp. 108-108.

215. Ibid., pl. 37; and see p. 141 point out the Iranian origin of this technique.

216. Ibid., pl. 38/21; and see p. 148 and following.

217. The grave belongs to the group of Hunnic princely tombs dated by J. Werner, Beiträge zur Archäologie..., p. 87, to the first half of the 5th century.

218. E. Salin, A. France-Lennord, Gallia, 14, 1, 1956, p. 69, fig. 9.

219. Ibid., p. 75; Al. Odobescu, Le trésor..., vol. I, p. 56, fig. 21.

220. F. Garscha, Germania, 20, 1936, pl. 38-39.

221. With regard to the close stylistic connection between the two pieces, see H. Arbmann, op.cit., p. 135; K. Böhner, op.cit., p. 231 and following although F. Garsche, op.cit., p. 196, states very clearly that the garnets of the sword from Altussheim are bulged ("mugelig geschliffen"), B. Arrhenius, op.cit., p. 119, considers them as being thin, similar to those of the sword found at Planig, see P. T. Kessler, MainzerZ, 35, 1940, p. 3, fig. 3/1, but according to the information known by us, this is not confirmed. The polychrome style of the sword from Planig, because of the cloisonné (in the shape of an umbo) ("mit halbkreisförmiger Ausbuchtung") cannot be connected with that of the sword from Althussheim.

222. F. Garsche, op.cit., p. 196 and following.

223. K. Böhner, op.cit., p. 224 and following.

224. As regards the analogies existing in the South of USSR, we mention the sword found at Kerch, Hospital Street, which is dated by a coin of Valentinian I or II (?); ibid., p. 225, fig. 2/1, or that discovered at Taman, ibid., p. 225, fig. 2/4, which have stylistic analogies with the collar with hinge. According to the chronology of the antiquities of Crimea, established by A. K. Ambroz, SA, 2, 1971, pp. 92-123 and fig. 2/25 the swords are dated to the first half of the 5th century.

225. J. Werner, op.cit., p. 88.

226. V. Bierbrauer, Die ostgotischen Grab- und Schatzfunde aus Italien, Biblioteca degli "Studi Medievali", vol. 7 (1974), p. 75 and following; ibid., p. 176, note 285; ibid., pl. 10/2-2; (the gold bracelet from Desana); ibid., pl. 12/2-2b (the gold bull from Desana); ibid., pl. 33/9 the cross worked in the same technique and found at Reggio Emilia; the cross dates from the end of the 5th century and the beginning of the following.

227. See supra, note 220.

228. J. Hubert, J. Pocher, W. F. Volbach, op.cit., p. 363; p. 220, fig. 233; p. 221, fig. 234; see also Al. Odobescu, Le trésor..., I, p. 56, fig. 20.

229. B. Arrhenius, op.cit., p. 119.

230. J. Werner, KölnerJahrb, 3, 1958, pl. 11/3; p. 57.

231. B. Schmidt, Die späte Völkerwanderungszeit in Mitteldeutschland, Berlin 1970 (Katalog), pl. 83; for the chronology of the group idem, Die späte Völkerwanderungszeit in Mitteldeutschland, Halle, 1961, p. 90, fig. 49.

232. F. Garsche, op.cit., p. 196.

233. J. Hubert, J. Pocher, W. F. Volbach, op.cit., p. 220, fig. 232; p. 363.

234. J. Nemeskéri, ArhErt, 5-6, 1944-1945, pl. 97.

235. L. Schmidt, Die Ostgermanen, München, 1969, p. 227.

236. Ibid., p. 227, note 5.

237. C. Preda, SCIVA, 26, 4, 1975, p. 446 and following.

238. L. Schmidt, op.cit., p. 228.

239. D. Hoffmann, Das spätrömische Bewegungsheer und die Notitia Dignitatum, Düsseldorf, 1969, p. 214.

240. Ibid., p. 391.

241. L. Schmidt, op.cit., p. 230.

242. E. Thompson, Latomus, 21, 1962, pp. 505-519.

243. S. Dolinescu-Ferche, On socio-economic relations between natives and Huns at the lower Danube, in vol. Relations between the autochtonous populations on the territory of Romania, Bucharest, 1975, p. 92; Acta sanctorum, II 3 (=962); Izvoarele istoriei Rômaniei, vol. 2, Bucharest, 1970: "Some of the natives, offering sacrifices to the gods in that village, were put to the test, as is usual with the Goths, and swore that nobody was Christian in their village".

244. E. Thompson, op.cit., p. 509.

245. Ibid., p. 531.

246. L. Várady, Das Letzte Jahrhundert Pannoniens, Budapest, 1969, p. 27.

247. Ibid., loc.cit.

248. L. Schmidt, op.cit., p. 231; Ammianus Marcellinus, XXXVII, 4; Zosimus, I, 11 (edition from Izvoarele istoriei României, vol. 2, Bucharest, 1970).

249. The discussion of the chronology L. Várady, op.cit., p. 27 and note 36.

250. Ibid., p. 29.

251. D. Hoffmann, op.cit., p. 429.

252. L. Várady, op.cit., p. 25 and following.

253. L. Schmidt, op.cit., p. 404; L. Varady, op.cit., p. 30.

254. Al. Odobescu, Le trésor..., vol. III, p. 20 and following; I. Nestor, in Istoria României, Bucharest, 1960, p. 698.

255. L. Schmidt, op.cit., p. 418; L. Várady, op.cit., p. 518.

256. L. Várady, op.cit., p. 27.

257. One of this kind of ethnic groups is that led by Alatheus and Saphrax.

258. Ibid., p. 75, with the whole bibliography and discussion concerning this problem.

259. Ibid., p. 89 and following.

260. Ibid., p. 193.

261. Ibid., p. 223 and following; Gh. Poenaru-Bordea, V. Barbu, Dacia, N.S., XIV, 1970, 251-295.

262. L. Várady, op.cit., p. 235.

263. R. Vulpe, I. Barnea, Din istoria Dobrogei, vol. II, Bucharest, 1968, p. 407.

264. I. Nestor, op.cit., p. 699; Gh. Poenaru-Bordea, V. Barbu, op.cit., p. 291 and following.

265. L. Várady, op.cit., p. 259 and following and especially p. 260.

266. L. Várady, op.cit., p. 22 and following.

267. Ibid., p. 148 and following.

268. J. Harmatta, ActaArchHung, 2, 1972, p. 227 and following.
R. Harhoiu, Aspects of the socio-political situation in Transylvania during the 5th century, in Relations between the autochtonous populations and the migratory population on the territory of Romania, Bucharest, 1975, p. 99 and following: S. Dolinescu-Ferche, op.cit., p. 91 and following.

269. Ibid., p. 322; N. Iorga, Istoria românilor, vol. II, Bucharest, 1936, p. 190.

270. J. Werner, Beiträge zur Archaölogie..., p. 66.

271. K. Horedt, Germania, 50, 1972, 1-2, p. 217 and following.

272. F. Lot, Les invasions germaniques. La pénétrations mutuelle du monde barbare et du monde romain, Paris, 1935, p. 103.

273. This tendency is very strongly attested by the clauses of the treaty of 433. The title of magister militum bestowed on Attila attests the effort of the imperial government to consolidate the image of the territorial unity of the Empire; see L. Várady, op.cit., p. 309.

274. In this context we mention an idea, accepted by more and more historians and archaeologists, that some of the princely tombs from the first half of the 5th century represent the archaeological response of barbarian federates who were members of the tribal aristocracy in the service of the Empire; see in this respect R. Pusztai, op.cit., p.114-115; L. Várady, op.cit., pp. 498-499; G. Mészáros, op.cit., p. 92; H. Vetters, Zum Problem der Kontinuität im neiderösterreichischen Limesgebiet, in Festschrift zum 70. Geburtstag von A. Klaar u. H. Mitscha-Mährheim, Jahrbuch für Landeskunde von Niederösterreich, 38, 1970, pp. 48-75; J. Tejral, op.cit., p. 57.

APPENDIX

CATALOGUE OF GOLD PIECES FROM THE 5th CENTURY FOUND IN THE TERRITORY OF ROMANIA
(See Fig. 8)

1. Apahida, district Cluj, Grave 1, J. Hampel, Alterthümer des frühen Mittelalters in Ungarn, Brauschweig, 1905, vol. 2 (1905), p. 39 and following; vol. 3 (1905), pl. 21-25. Grave 2, K. Horedt, D. Protase, Germania, 50, 1-2, 1972, 174-220.

2. Balaci, district Teleorman, isolated find (bracelet with slightly thickened terminals, semi-circular pectoral, piece of round wire) S. Dolinescu-Ferche, SCIV, 14, 1, 1963, pp. 183-

3. Bălteni, district Galaţi, inhumation burial, I. T. Dragomir, SCIV, 17, 1, 1966, 181.

4. Braşov, district Braşov, Isolated find (finger-ring with the bezel in the shape of a bulls-head). J. Hampel, op.cit., vol. 2 (1905), p. 59; vol. 3 (1905), pl. 50/4. Isolated find (shoe-buckle). E. Beninger, Der westgotisch-analische Zug nach Mitteleuropa (Manmus-bibliothek 51), Leipzig, 1931, p. 32, fig. 8.

5. Buhăieni, com. Andrieşeni, district Iaşi, Grave, A. Florescu, Dacia, N.S., 4, 1960, p. 561 and following.

6. Buneşti, district Braşov, Isolated find (collar with loop and hook for fastening, K. Horedt, Germania, 25, 1941, p. 121, pl. 21/10.

7. Cepari, com. Dumitrana, district Bitriţa-Năsăud, Grave, D. Protase, Dacia, N.S., 4, 1960, p. 569 and following.

8. Chiojd, district Buzău, Grave, C. C. Giurescu, RIR, 5-6, 1935-1936, 331-347; p. 336, fig. 2.

9. Cîlnău, district Buzău, Isolated find: shoe-buckle (unpublished). The collection of the History Museum of Romania, see Al. Odobescu, Le trésor..., vol. I, p. 479, fig. 192.

10. Cluj, district Cluj, Stray find: two ear-rings with massive polyhedron cube, G. László, Közlemények, 1, 1941, p. 127; p. 124, pl. 1/10, 11.

11. Cluj-Someşeni, district Cluj, Hoard, K. Horedt, D. Protase, Germania, 48, 1-2, 1970, 89-98.

12. Conceşti, district Botoşani, Grave, C. Bloşiu, Cercetări istorice, Iaşi, 5, 1974, pp. 59-81, with the whole older bibliography.

13. Dulceanca, com. Vedea, Grave, V. Dumitrescu, Dacia, N.S., 5, 1961, p. 537 and following.

14. Fîntînele, com. Matei, district Bistriţa-Năsăud, Graves, S. Morintz, Dacia, N.S., 17, 1973, p. 375 and information I. H. Crişan.

15. Gheräseni, district Buzău, Grave, information Gh. Diaconu.

16. Hunedoara, district Hunedoara, Isolated find: two ear-rings with polyhedron cube decorated with almandines. G. László, op.cit., p. 127; p. 124, pl. 1/8, 9.

17. Izvin, com. Recaş, district Timiş, Isolated find: ear-ring with polyhedron cube decorated with almandines. D. Csallany, ArchHung, 38, 1961, p. 195, pl. 218/4.

18. Mediaş, district Sibiu, Isolated find: ear-ring with polyhedron cube decorated with almandines. K. Horedt, Germania, 25, 1941, p. 123, pl. 21/8.

19. Periam, district Timiş, Grave, J. Hampel, A rěggip kŏzep kor (IV-X. század) Emlekei Magyar homban, Budapest, 1894, vol. 1, pl. VI-VII.

20. Pietroasele, district Buzău.

21. Pîrscov, district Buzău, hoard, V. Teodorescu, Bucharest, Materiale de istorie şi muzeografie, 9, 1972, p. 91, note 47 (unpublished). Collection of the History Museum of Romania.

22. Rotopăneşti, com. Horodniceni, district Suceava, Fragment of pendant found in a level of the 2nd-3rd centuries. E. Busuioc, Dacia, N.S., 17, 1973,

23. Simleul Silvaniei, district Sălaj, Two hoards, J. Hampel, op.cit., vol. 2 (1905), p. 15 and following; vol. 3 (1905), pl. 14-31; N. Fettich, ArchHung, 8, 1932.

24. Transilvania. Isolated find: bracelet with thickened terminals. G. László, op.cit., p. 125; p. 123, fig. 1/3.

25. Uileacul Simleului, district Sălaj, Isolated find: collar with hook for fastening, ArhErt, 22, 1902, p. 432.

26. Veţel, suburb of the town Deva, district Hunedoara, Grave, G. László, op.cit., p. 124 and following; pl. 124, pl. 1/1-7.

FINDS OF GOLD PIECES OF THE FIFTH CENTURY

1. Apahida, district Cluj
2. Balaci, district Teleorman
3. Bălteni, district Buzău
4. Braşov, district Braşov
5. Buhăieni, com. Andrieşeni, district Iaşi
6. Buneşti, district Braşov
7. Cepari, com. Dumitra, district Bistriţa-Năsăud
8. Chiojhd, district Buzău
9. Cîlnău, district Buzău
10. Cluj, district Cluj

11. Cluj-Someşeni, district Cluj
12. Conceşti, district Botoşani
13. Dulceanca, com. Vedea, district Teleorman
14. Fîntînele, com. Matei, district Bistriţa-Năsăud
15. Gherăseni, district Buzău
16. Hunedoara, district Hunedoara
17. Izvin, com. Recaş, district Timiş
18. Mediaş, district Sibiu
19. Periam, district Timiş
20. Pietroasele, district Buzău
21. Pîrscov, district Buzău
22. Rotopaneşti, com. Horodniceni, district Suceava
23. Simleul Silvaniei, district Sălaj
24. Uileacul Simleului, district Sălaj
25. Veţel, suburb Deva, district Hunedoara

GOLD COIN FINDS OF THE FOURTH CENTURY

1. Biled, district Timiş
2. Borsec, district Harghita
3. Denta, district Timiş
4. Deta, district Timiş
5. Dolheşti, district Suceava
6. Carani, district Timiş
7. Crasna, district Suceava
8. Curcani, district Ilfov
9. Feldioara, district Braşov
10. Moigrad, com. Mirşid, district Sălaj
11. Orşova, district Caraş-Severin
12. Retiş, district Sibiu
13. Rogova, district Mehedinţi
14. Simleul Silvaniei, district Sălaj
15. Valea Strîmbă, district Harghita

GOLD COIN FINDS OF THE FIFTH CENTURY

16. Aiton, district Cluj
17. Cepari, com. Dumitra, district Bistriţa-Năsăud
18. Cig, com. Tăşnad, district Satu Mare
19. Ciorogîrla, district Ilfov
20. Cluj-Napoca, district Cluj
21. Copalnic-Mănăştur, district Maramureş
22. Doba Mică, com. Dobrin, district Sălaj
23. Dobra, district Hunedoara
24. Dolheşti, district Suceava
25. Domneşti, district Ilfov
26. Hida, district Sălaj
27. Holboca, district Iaşi
28. Iernut, district Mureş

29. Luduş, district Mureş
30. Luna de Jos,. com. Dăbîca, **district Cluj**
31. Mirosloveşti, district Iaşi
32. Moroda, district Arad
33. Meşindorf, com. Buneşti, **district Braşov**
34. Ocna Sibiului, district Sibiu
35. Petroman, district Timiş
36. Răscruci, com. Bonţida, **district Cluj**
37. Sebeş, district Alba
38. Sînpaul, district Harghita
39. Suceava, district Suceava
40. Valea lui Mihai, **district Bihor**
41. Văsaş, com. Neaua, **district Mureş**

ABBREVIATIONS

Aarbger	Aarbger for nordisk Oldkyndighed og Historie, København.
ActaArch	Acta Archaeologica Academica Scientarum Hungaricae, Budapest.
AISC	Anuarul Institutului de Studii Clasice, Cluj.
AMN	Acta Musei Napocensis, Cluj.
Analele rom-sov	Analele româno-sovietice, Bucharest.
ArchHung	Archaeologia Hungarica, Budapest.
ArhErt	Archaeologiai Ertesitö, Budapest.
Archeologija Kiev	Archeologija Kiev, Institut Arheologii, Kiev.
ArhPam	Arheologicni Pam'jatky URSR, Kiev.
Arrabona	Arrabona, Györ.
BayerVbl	Bayerische Vorgeschichtsblätter, München.
BerRGR	Bericht der Römisch-Germanischen Komission, Frankfurt am Main.
BonnerJahrb	Bonner Jahrbücher, Bonn.
Carpica	Carpica, Bacău.
Dacia	Dacia, Revue d'archéologie et d'histoire ancienne, Bucharest, I-XII, 1924-1944; N.S. I, 1957
DolgCluj	Dolgozatok-Travaux de la Section Numismatique et Archéologique du Musée National de Transylvanie, Cluj.
FoliaArch	Folia Archaeologica, Budapest.
Fornvännen	Fornvännen. Tidskrift för svenska antikvarisk forskning, Stockholm.
Gallia	Gallia. Fouilles et Monuments archéologiques en France Metropolitaine, Paris.
Germania	Germania. Anzeiger der Römisch-Germanischen Komission des Deutschen Archäologischen Instituts, Berlin.
JahrbfAltertumskunde	Jahrbuch für Altertumskunde, Vienna

KölnerJahrb	Kölner Jahrbuch für Vor- und Frühgeschichte Köln..
MainzerZ	Mainzer Zeitschrift, Mainz.
Materiale	Materiale şi Cercetări Arheologice, Bucharest.
Meddellanden	Meddellanden från Lunds Universitets Historicks Museum, Lund.
Offa	Offa Berichte und Mitteilungen aus dem Schleswig-Holsteinschen Landesmuseum für Vor- und Frühgeschichte und dem Institut für Ur- und Frühgeschichte der Universität Kiel, Neumünster.
PamArch	Pamâtky Archeologické, Prague.
RESEE	Revue des Études Sud-Est Européenne, Bucharest.
RIR	Revista Istorică Romậna, Bucureşti 1932-1947.
SaalburgJahrb	Saalburg Jahrbuch, Berlin.
SCIVA	Studii si Cercetări de Istorie Veche şi Arheologie, Bucharest.
SlovArch	Slovenská Archaeologia, Nitra.
SA	Sovetskaia Archaeologia, Moscow.

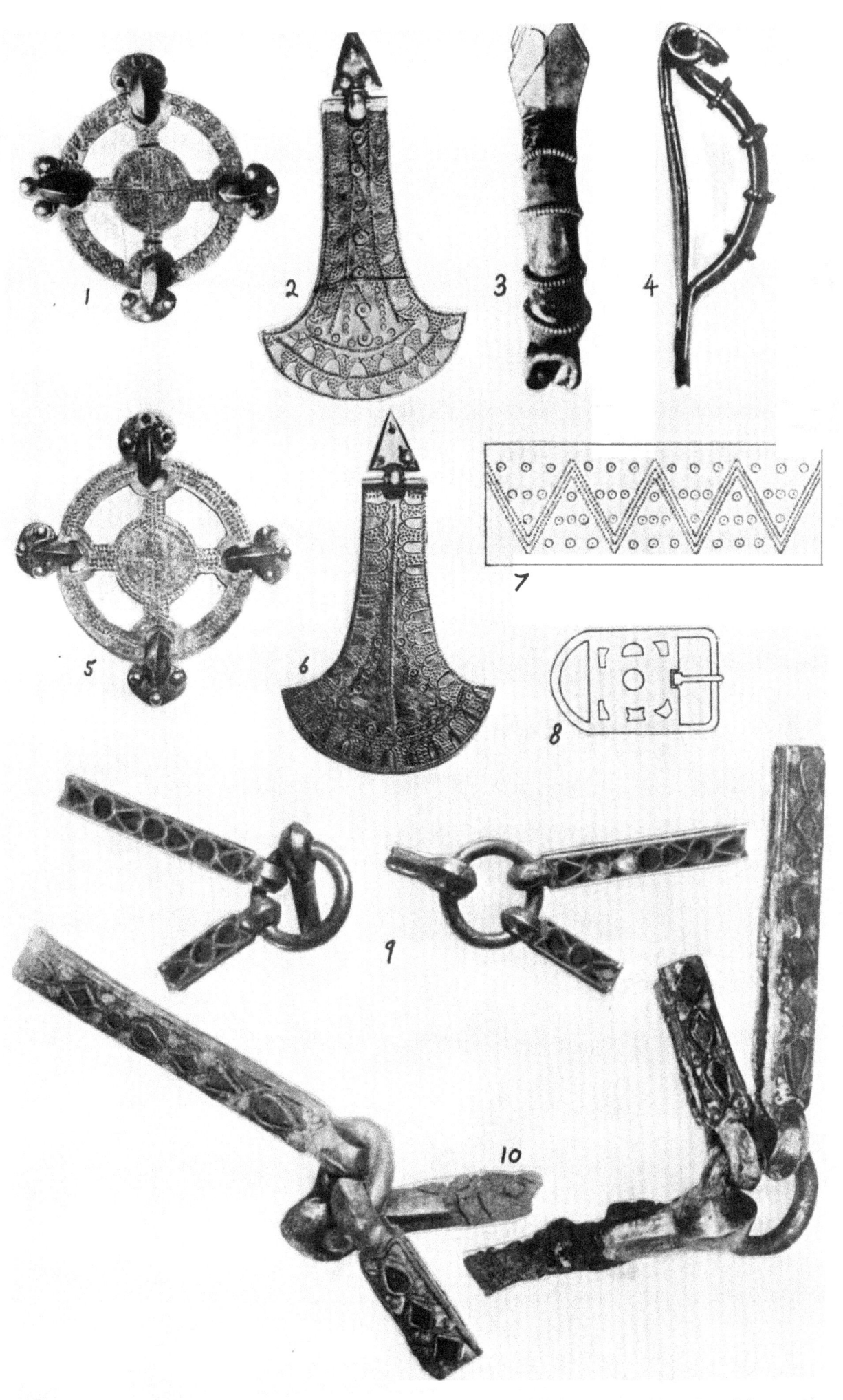

Fig. 1. 1-8: the hoard of Coșovenii de Jos; 9-10: pieces of harness

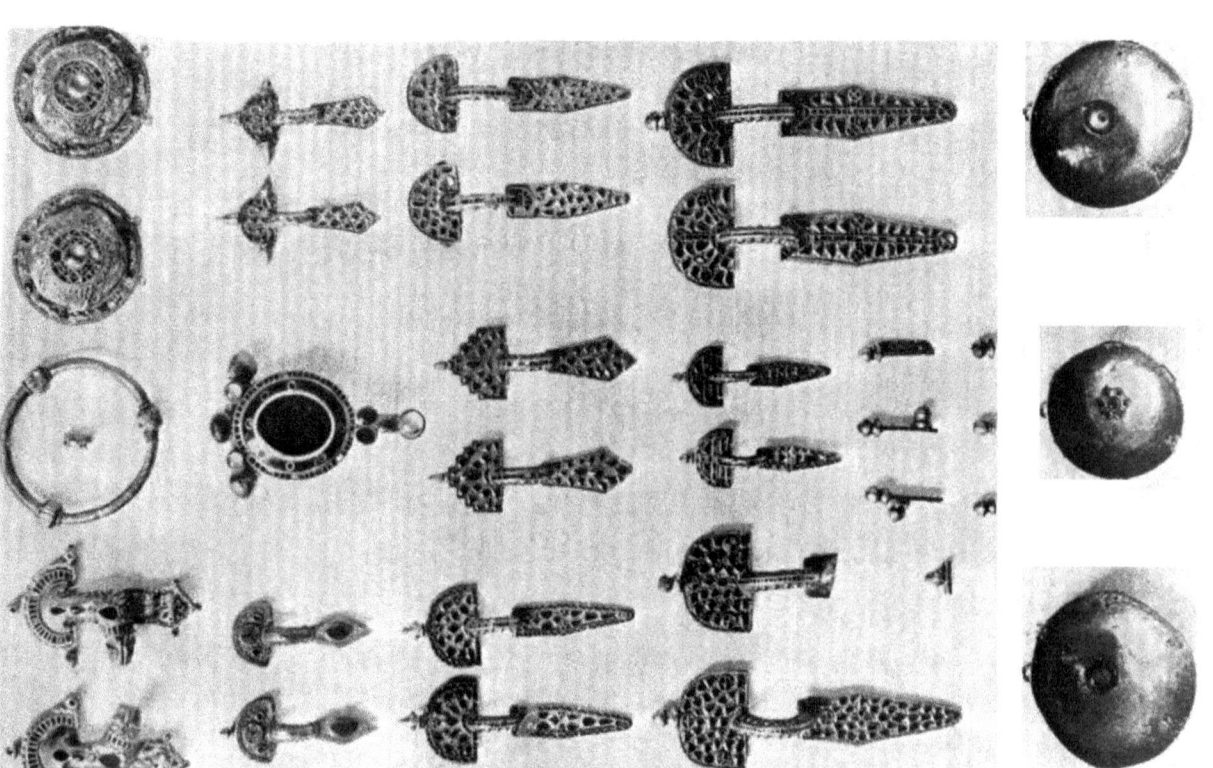

Fig. 2. 1: hoard 2 from Simleul Silvaniei; 2: hoard 1 from Simleul Silvaniei.

Fig. 3. Hoard 2 from Simleul Silvaniei; 1-1a: fibula with onyx; 2-2a: lion shaped fibula.

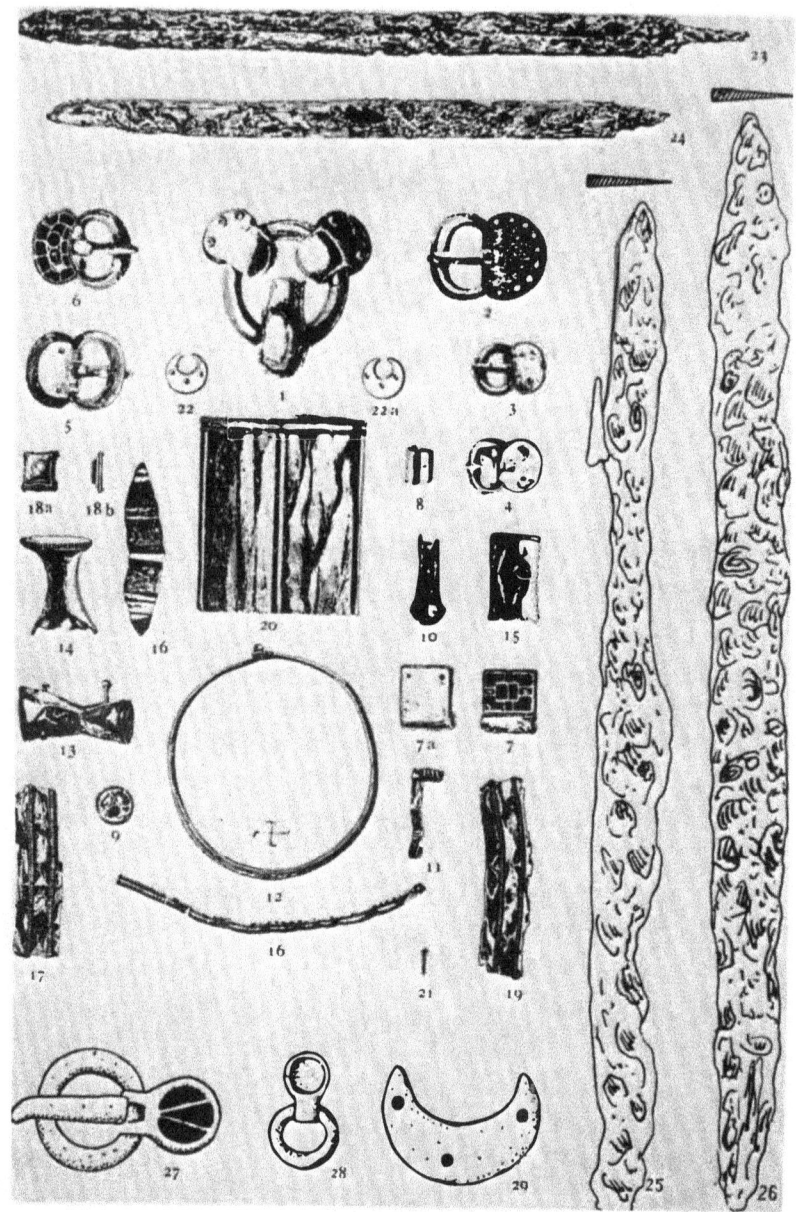
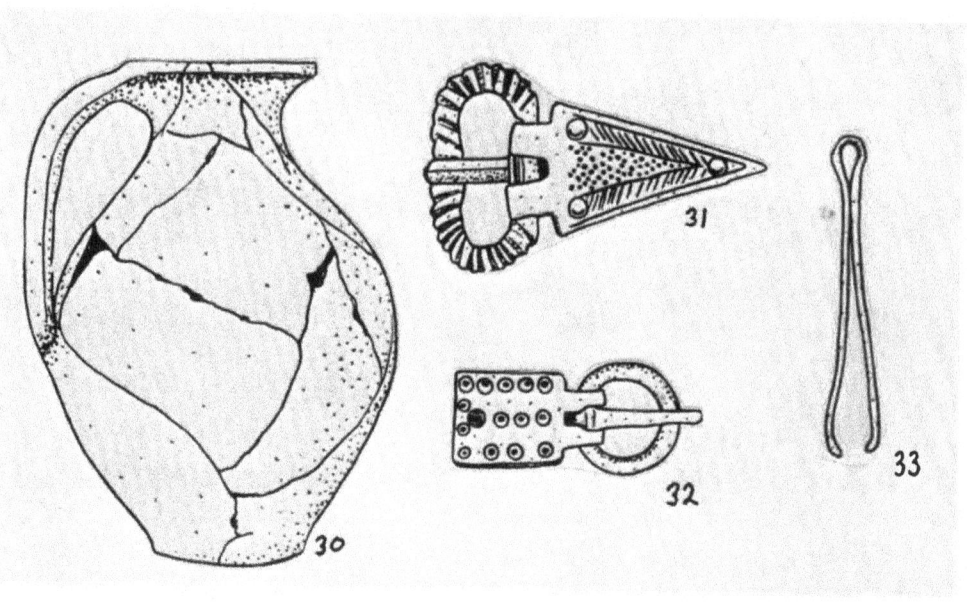

Fig. 4. 4-29: the grave-goods from the tomb found at Musliumova; 30-33: grave-goods of the tomb found at Gyöngyösapáti.

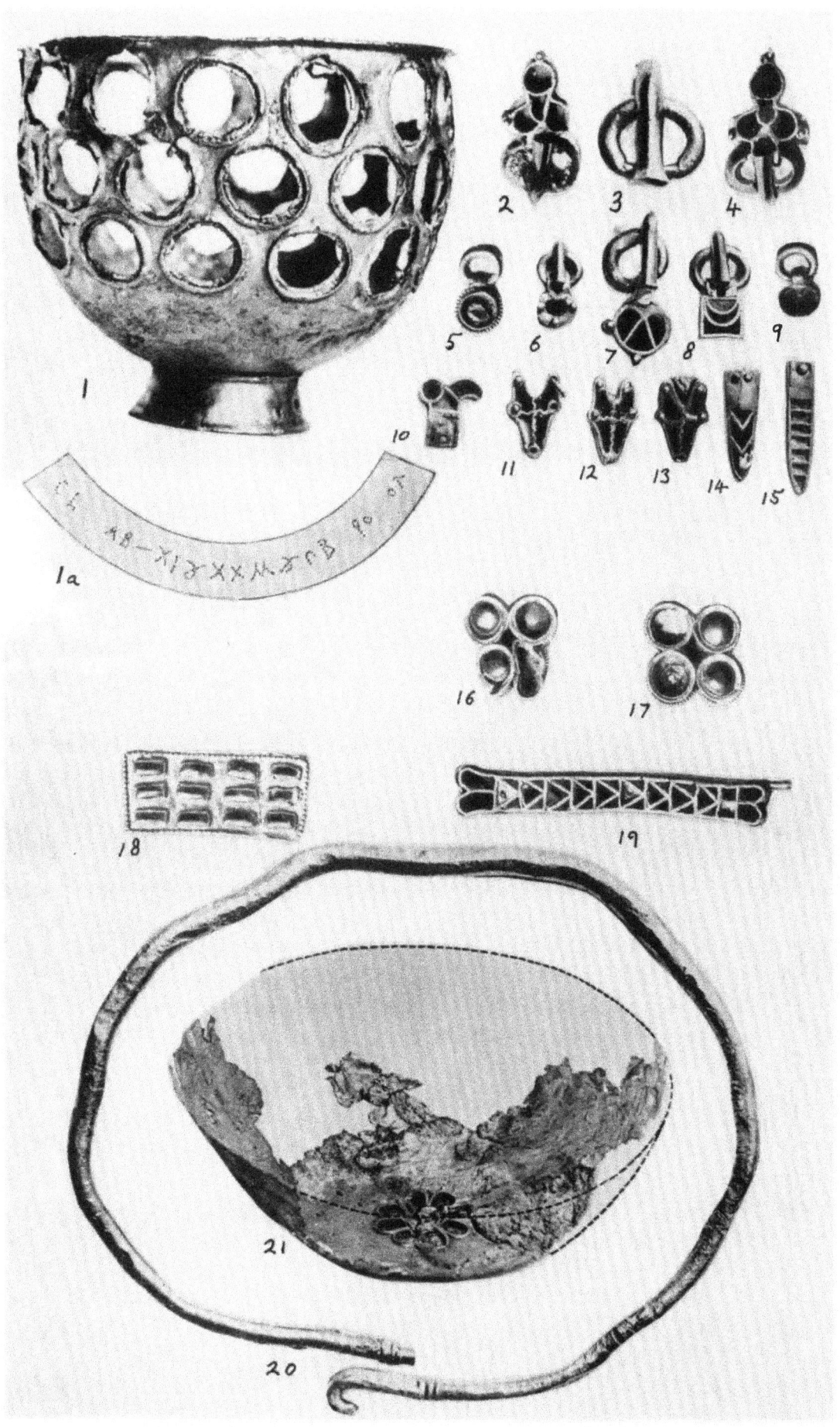

Fig. 5. 1-21: pieces belonging to the grave-goods of the princely tomb found at Széged-Nagyszéksós.

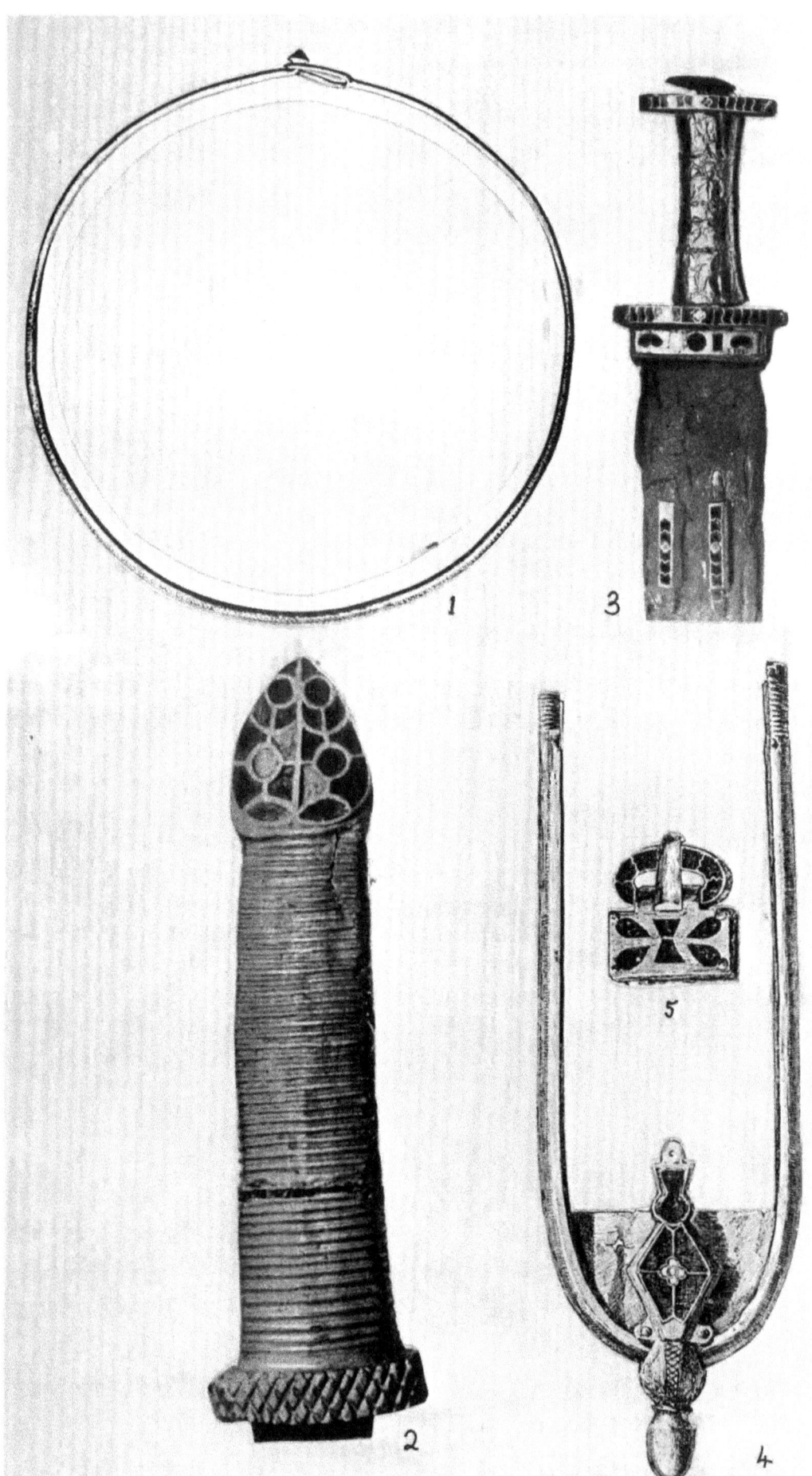

Fig. 6. 1-2: pieces belonging to the grave-goods of the princely tomb discovered at Pouan; sword from the princely tomb found at Flonheim; 4-5: spur and buckle from the grave discovered at Komarŏm.

Fig. 7. 1: dyptich from Halberstadt, detail; dyptich with the representation of Rome and Constantinople, detail, Kunsthistorisches Museum Vienna; 3: bust of Valentinian II (Magyar Nat. Museum), detail.

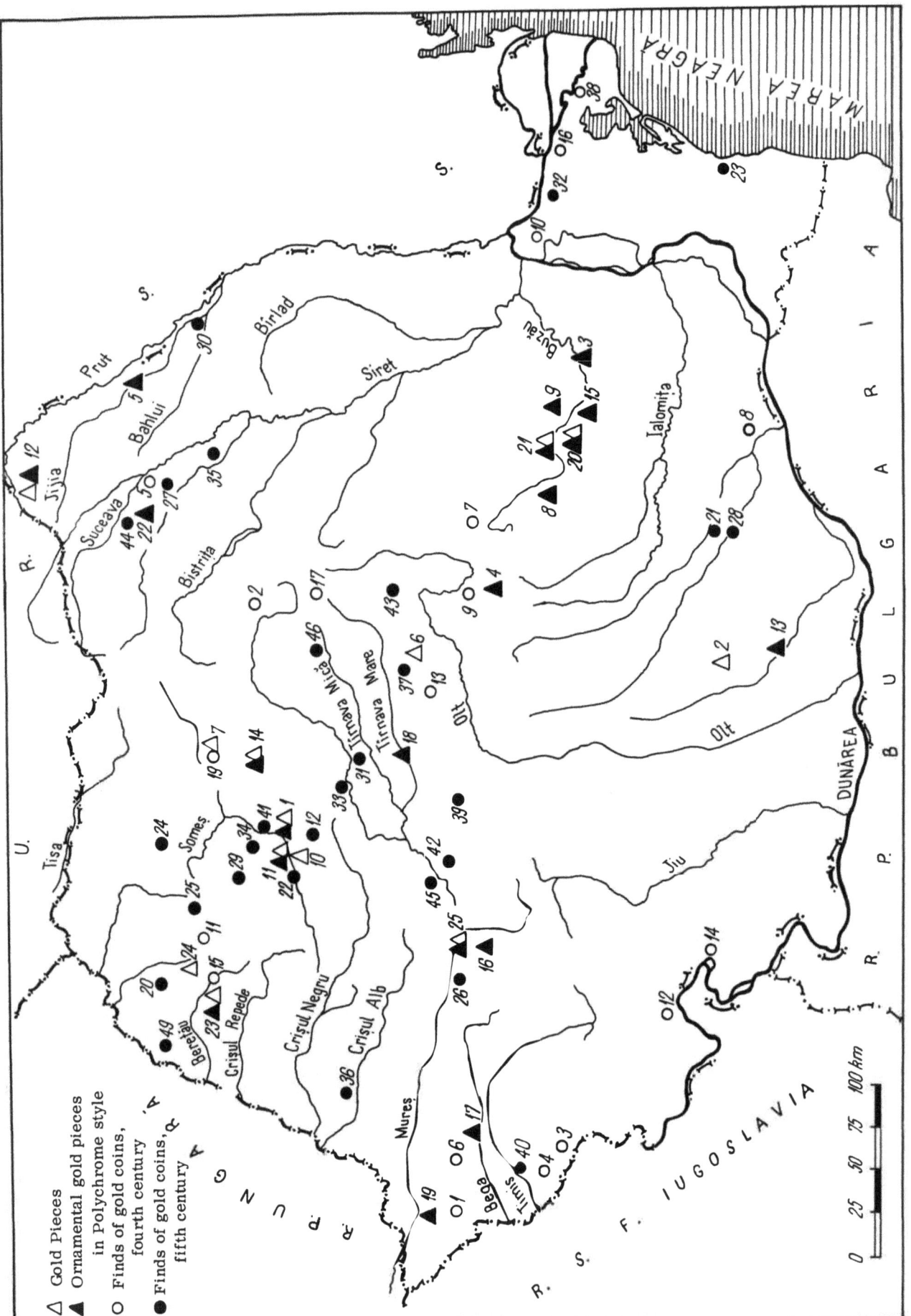

Fig. 8. Distribution-map of gold pieces and coin-finds from Romania.

No.	Site	Cabochon	Straight Cloisonné	Cloisonné à Jour	Fluted Garnets	Wavy Cloisonné
1	Bălteni	●				
2	Buhăeni	●				
3	Chiojd	●				
4	Dulceanca	●				
7	Gherăseni	●				
8	Pîrscov	●				
9	Rotopănești	●				
10	Vetel	●	●			
11	Concești	●	●			
12	Șimleul Silvaniei	●	●			
13	Brașov		●			
14	Cîlnău		●			
15	Hunedoara		●			
16	Periam		●			
17	Mediaș		●			
18	Izvin		●			
19	Pietroasa	●	●	●	●	
20	Someșeni	●	●	●		●
21	Apahida I	●	●		●	●
22	Apahida II		●		●	●

Fig. 9. Table of the combined gold-finds from Romania.

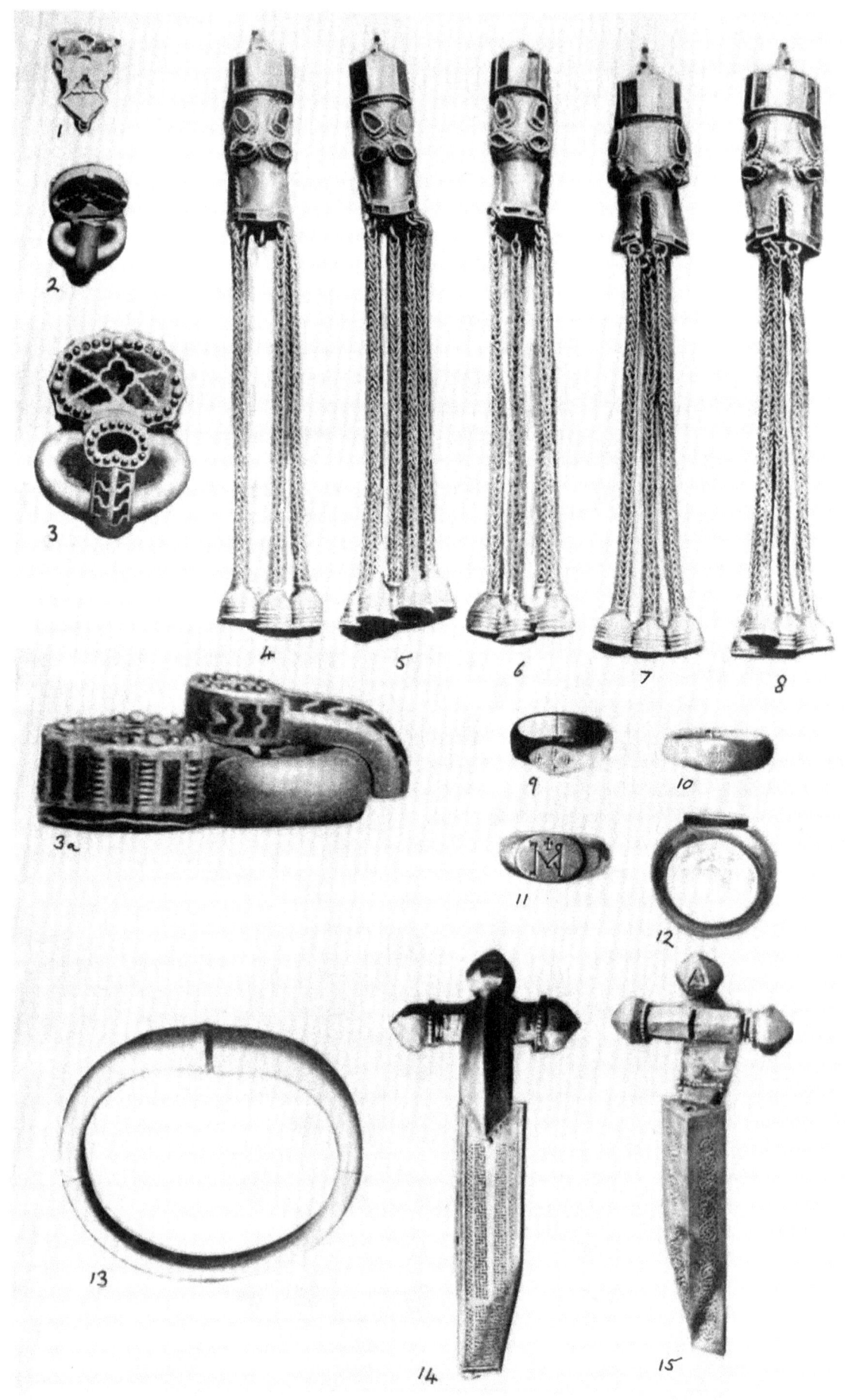

Fig. 10. Grave-goods from princely tomb 1 at Apahida.

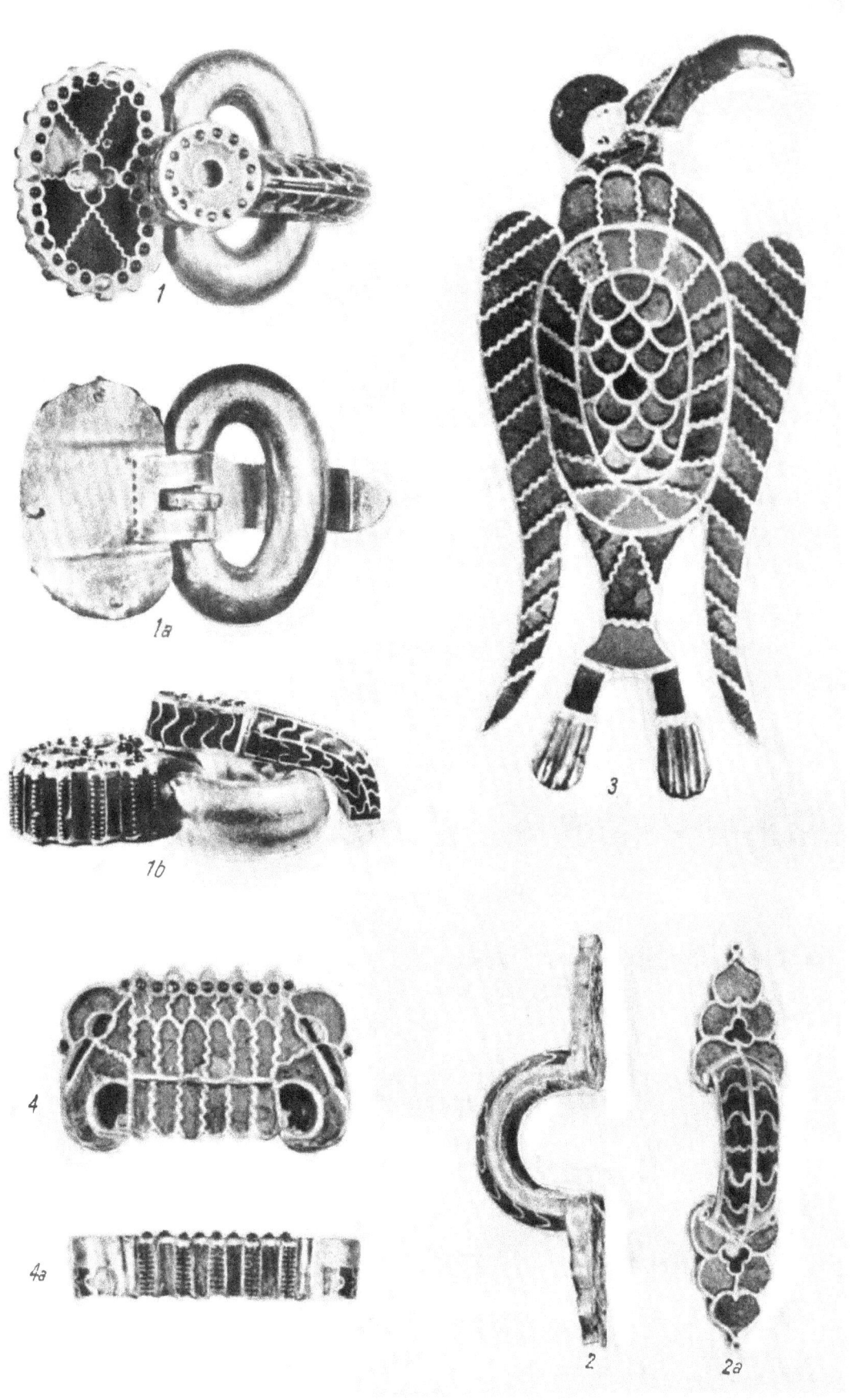

Fig. 11. Grave-goods from princely tomb 2 at Apahida.

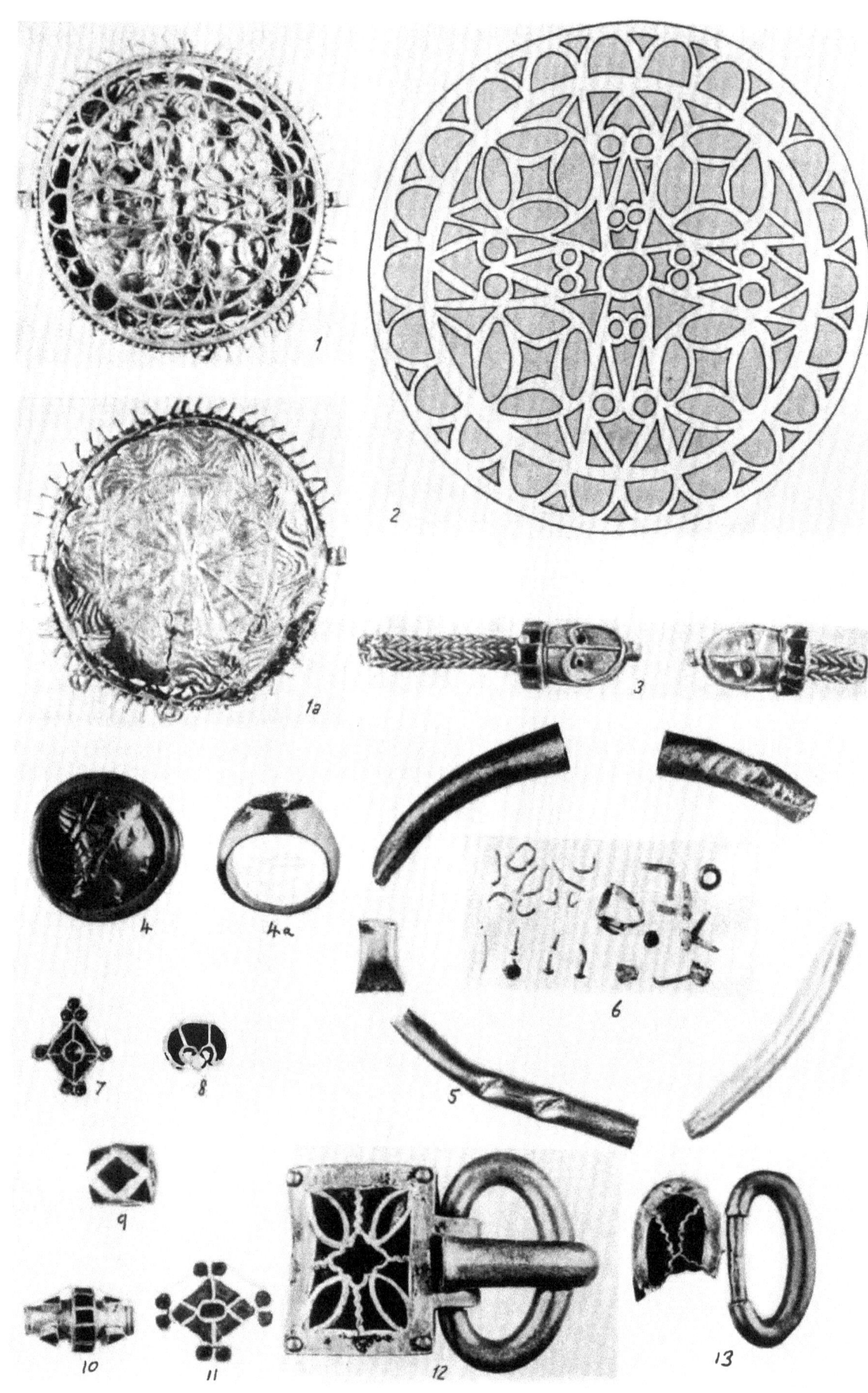

Fig. 12. Pieces from the Someşeni hoard.

Fig. 13. Grave-goods from the princely tomb at Unterseibenbrunn.

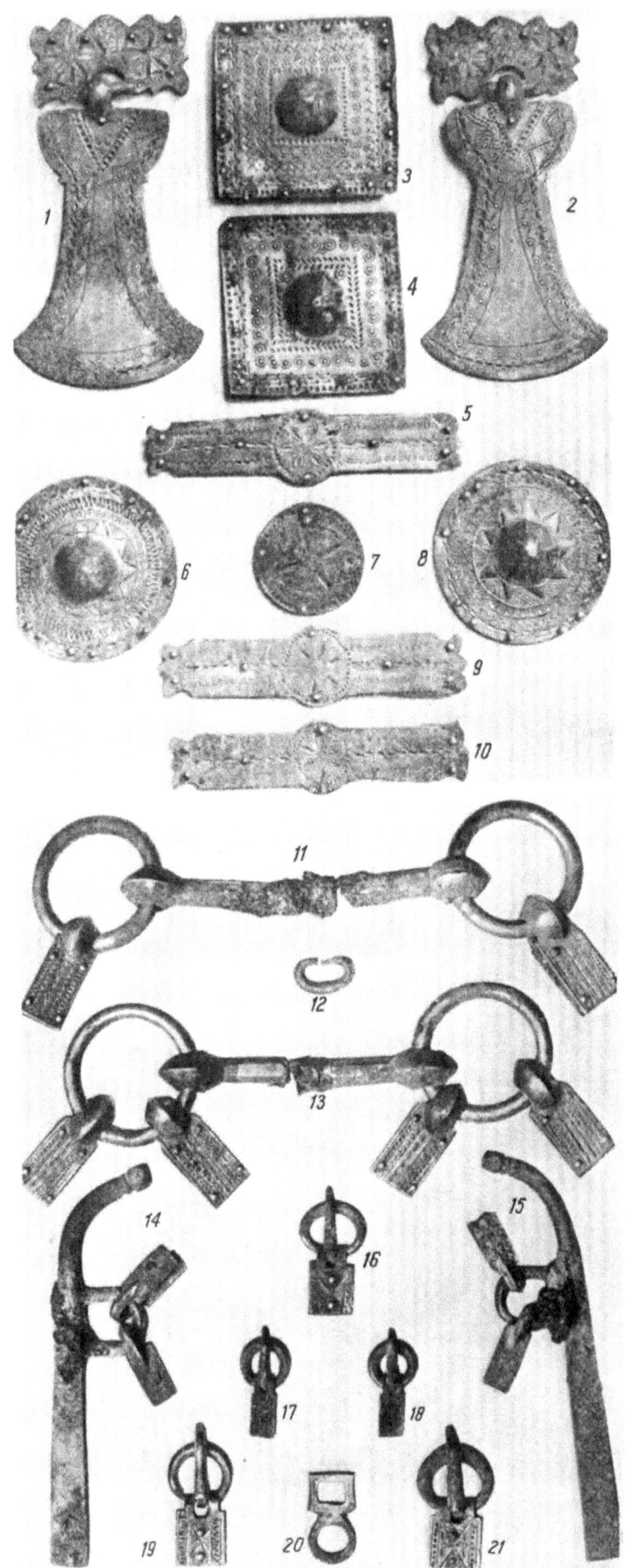

Fig. 14. Grave-goods from the princely tomb at Unterseibenbrunn.

Fig. 15. The princely tomb at Jakuszowice.

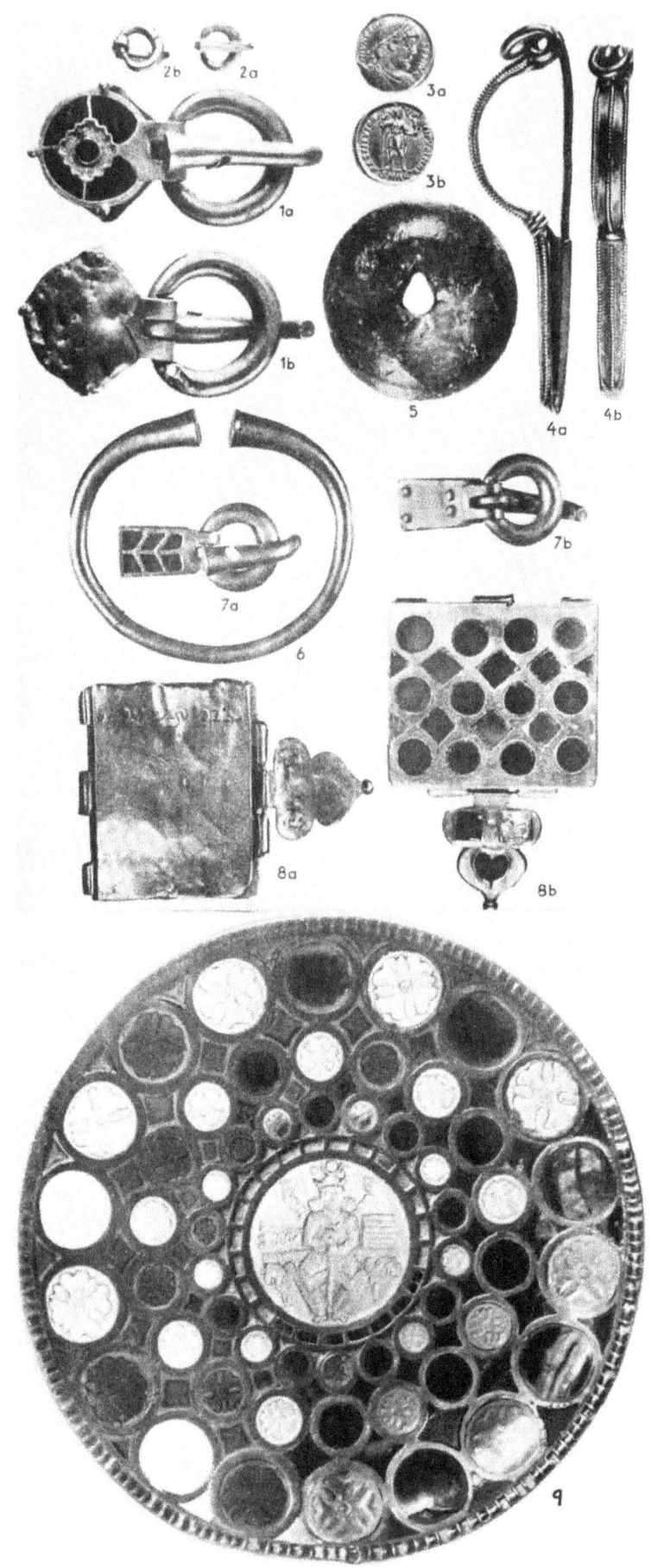

Fig. 16. 1-8: grave-goods from the tomb found at Wolfsheim:
9: the cup of Khusro Aparwez.

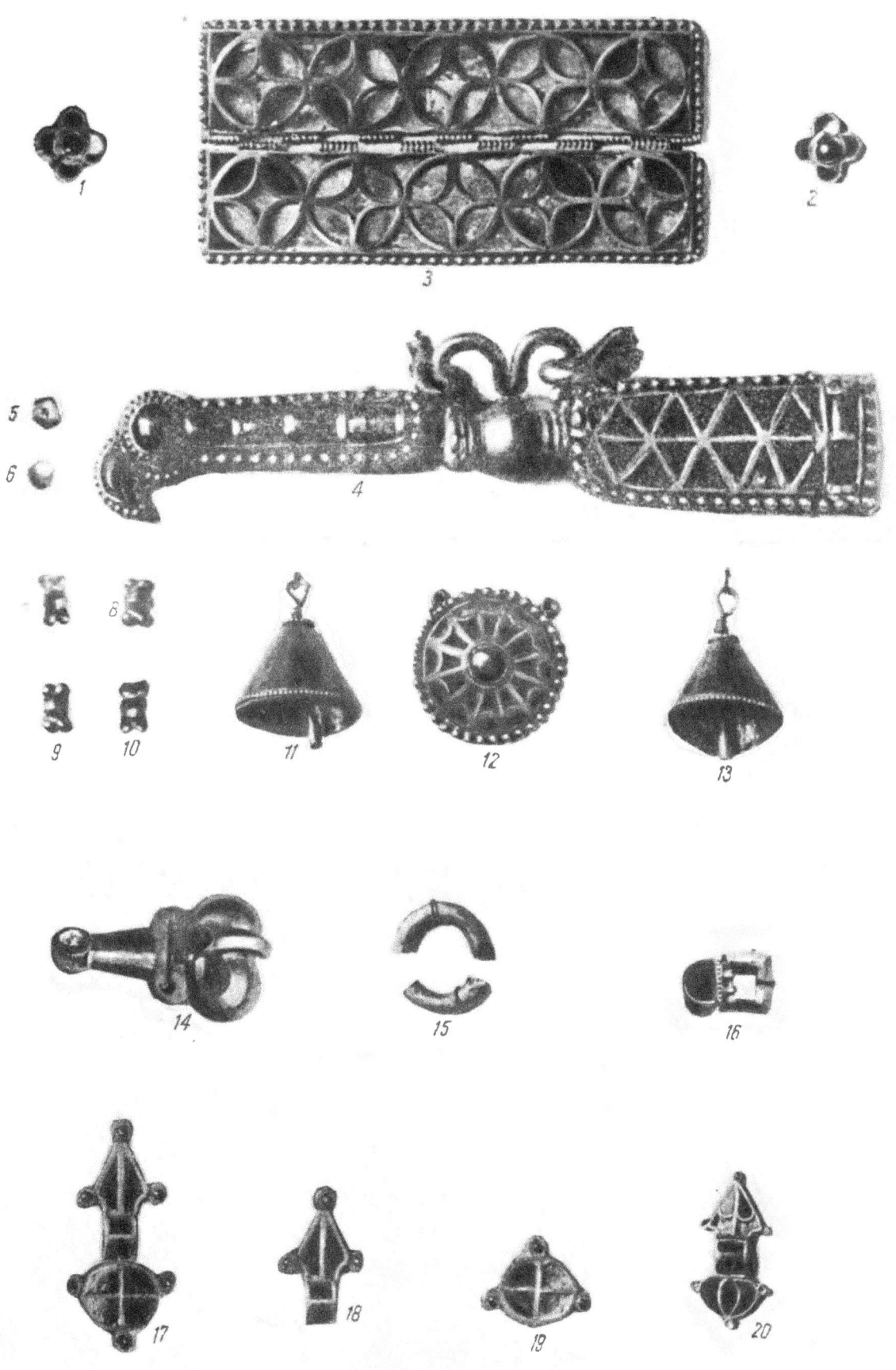

Fig. 17. The princely tomb from Kudinetov.

Fig. 18. 1-6: The grave-goods from the tomb discovered at Altlussheim; 7-7a: sword found at Kerch, Hospital Street; 8: fragment of sword from Taman.

Plate I. Pietroasa Treasure: Plate.

Plate II. Pietroasa Treasure: 1. Jug; 2. Detail of upper part; 3. Detail of rim.

Plate III. Pietroasa Treasure: Patera.

Plate IV. Pietroasa Treasure: Patera, central figure.

Plate V. Pietroasa Treasure: Patera (details).

Plate VI. Pietroasa Treasure: Patera (details).

Plate VII. Pietroasa Treasure: 1-2, 8-sided cup, 1. side view; 2. Details of handles.

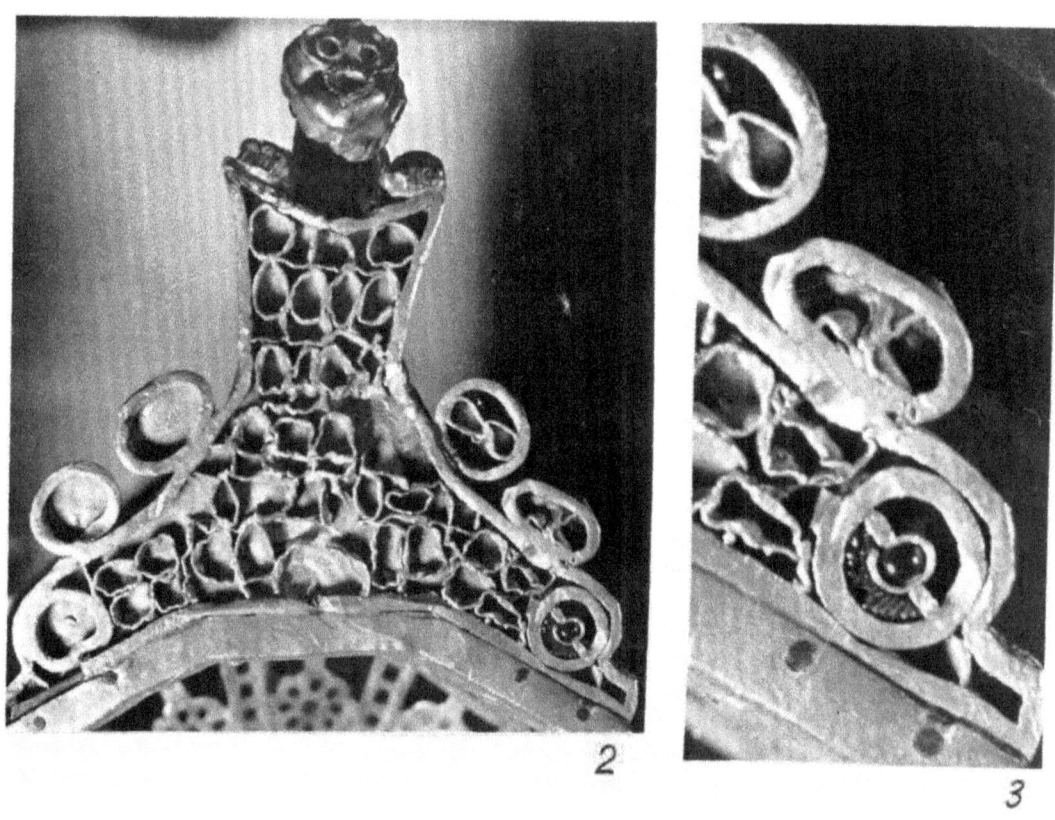

Plate VIII. Pietroasa Treasure: 1-3, 12-sided cup, 1. side view;
2. Details.

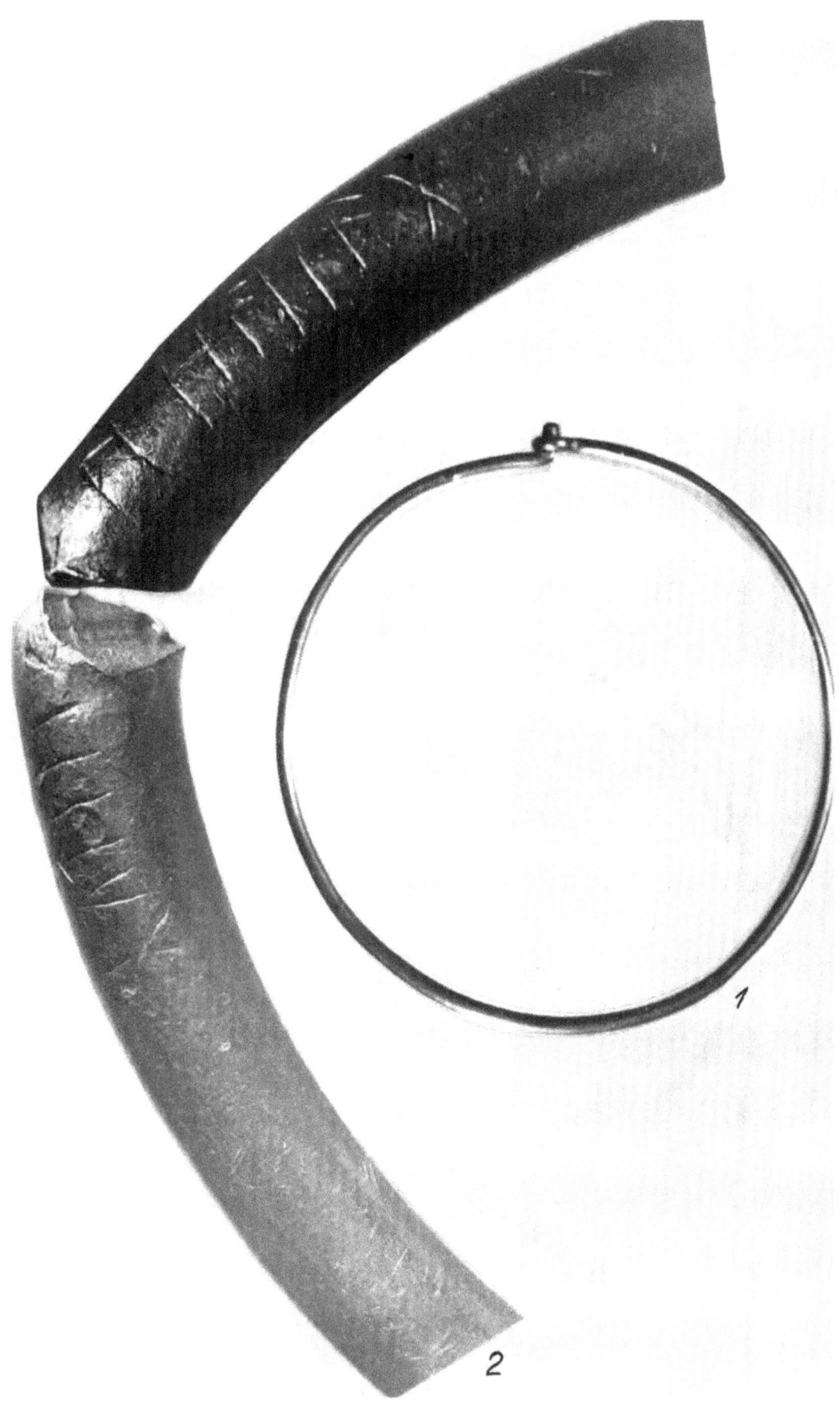

Plate IX. Pietroasa Treasure: 1. Plain collar; 2. Collar with inscription.

Plate X. Pietroasa Treasure: Hinged collar.

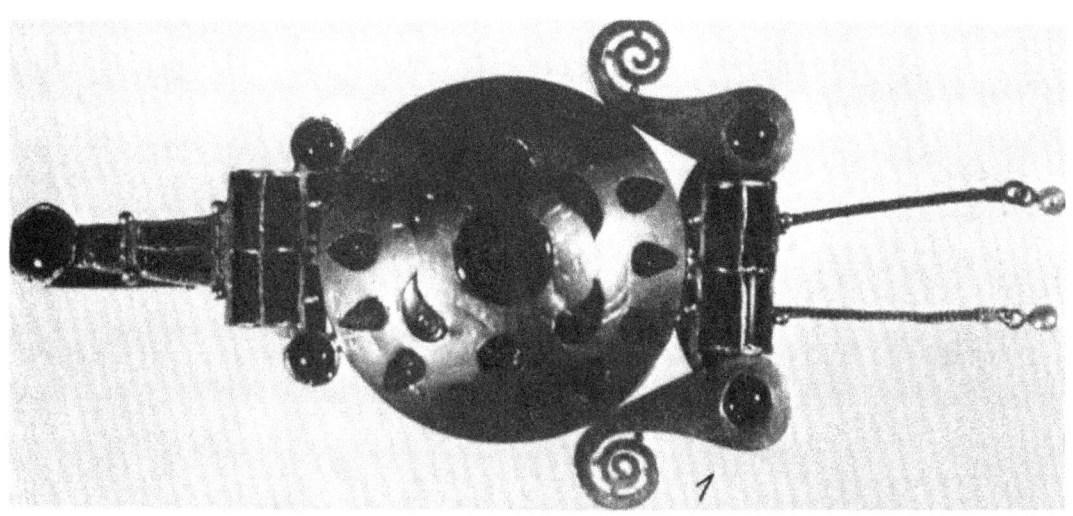

Plate XI: Pietroasa Treasure: 1-3, small fibula.

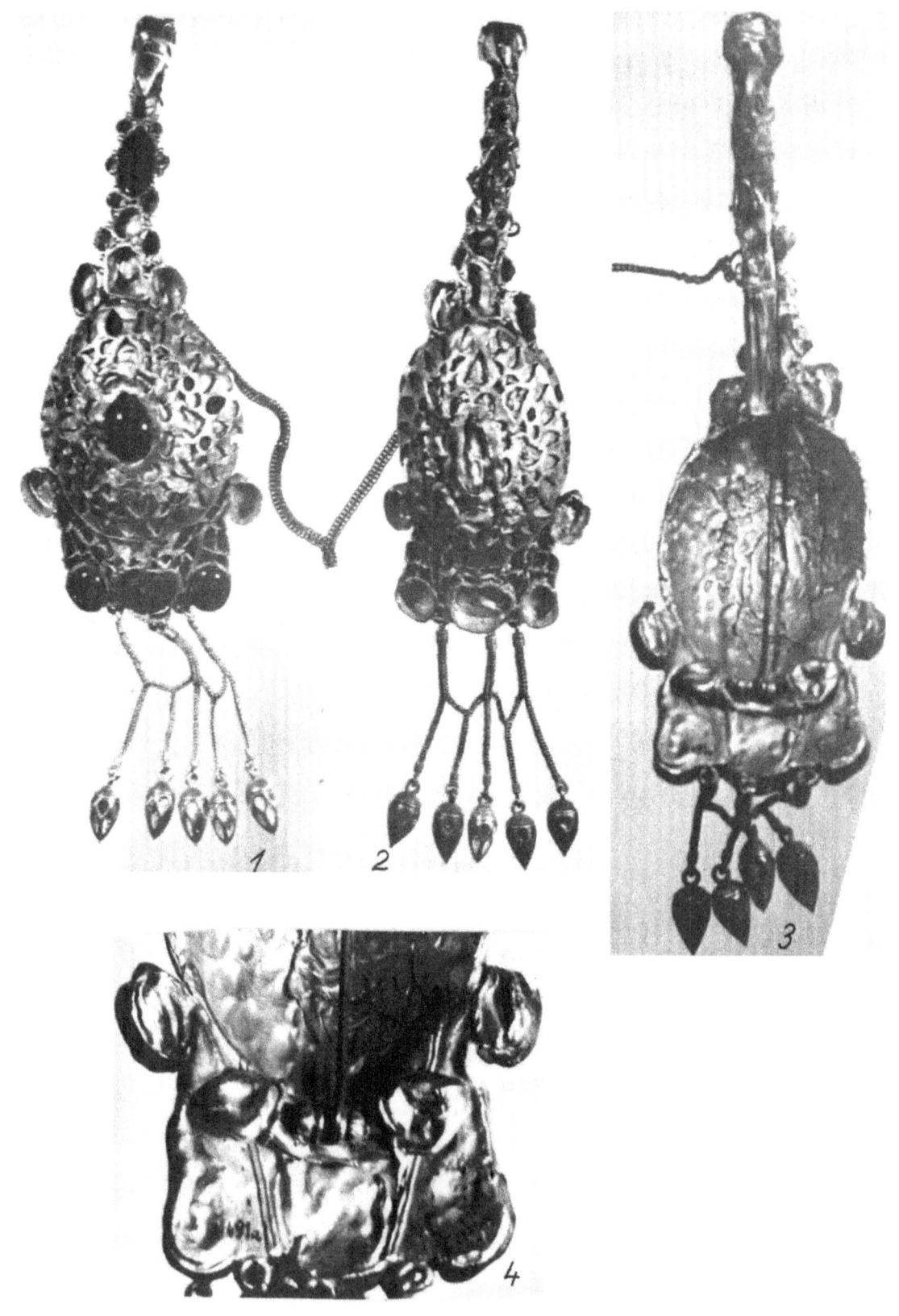

Plate XII. Pietroasa Treasure: 1-4, medium size fibulae.

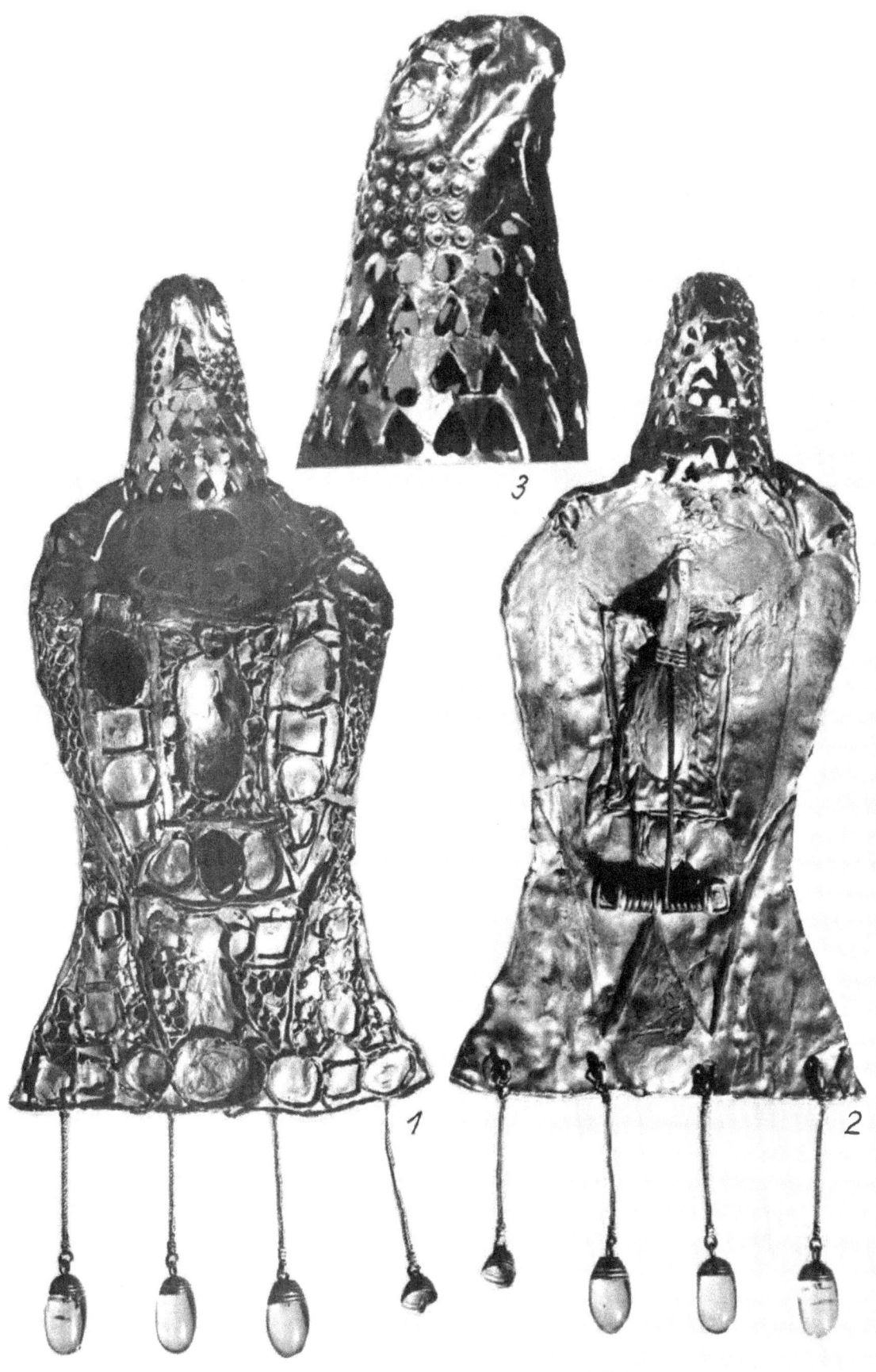

Plate XIII. Pietroasa Treasure: large fibula.